Ole Edvart Rölvaag

Twayne's United States Authors Series

Leif Sjöberg, Editor

State University of New York at Stony Brook

TUSAS 455

OLE EDVART RÖLVAAG
(1876–1931)
Photography courtesy of Ella Valborg Tweet

Ole Edvart Rölvaag

By Einar Haugen

Harvard University

Twayne Publishers • Boston

Ole Edvart Rölvaag

Einar Haugen

Copyright © 1983 by G. K. Hall & Company
All Rights Reserved
Published by Twayne Publishers
A Division of G. K. Hall & Company
70 Lincoln Street
Boston, Massachusetts 02111

Book Production by Marne B. Sultz

Book Design by Barbara Anderson

Printed on permanent/durable acid-free
paper and bound in the United States of
America.

Library of Congress Cataloging in Publication Data

Haugen, Einar Engvald, 1906–
   Ole Edvart Rölvaag.

   (Twayne's United States authors series; TUSAS 455)
   Bibliography: p. 148
   Includes index.
   1. Rölvaag, O. E. (Ole Edvart), 1876–1931—Criticism
and interpretation.   I. Title.   II. Series.
PT9150.R55Z59 1983   839.8'2372   83-5120
ISBN 0-8057-7395-9

In memory of my mother
KRISTINE HAUGEN (1878–1965)
Who first introduced me to
Ole Rölvaag, man and writer

Contents

About the Author

Einar Haugen is a scholar, writer, and educator in the field of Scandinavian languages and literature. He was Victor S. Thomas Professor of Scandinavian and Linguistics at Harvard University from 1964 until his retirement in 1975. Before that he was Torger Thompson and Vilas Professor at the University of Wisconsin, Madison, where he taught from 1931 to 1964. Born in Sioux City, Iowa, in 1906 of Norwegian parents, he took his B.A. at St. Olaf College in 1928 and his Ph.D. at the University of Illinois in 1931. He is known for his textbooks in Norwegian, including a *Norwegian-English Dictionary* for American students. In addition to numerous articles in scholarly journals, he has published *The Norwegian Language in America* (1953, 1969), *Bilingualism in the Americas* (1956), *Language Conflict and Language Planning* (1966), *The Ecology of Language* (1972), *The Scandinavian Languages* (1976), and *Ibsen's Drama: Author to Audience* (1979). He has traveled and lectured widely and has been honored by the Swedish and Norwegian governments as well as by a number of American and Scandinavian universities and scientific academies. He has been president of the Society for Advancement of Scandinavian Studies, of the Linguistic Society of America, and of the Tenth International Congress of Linguists.

Preface

Ole Edvart Rølvaag, or O. E. Rölvaag, as he wrote his name on the English translations of his books, burst upon the American literary scene in 1927 like a meteor out of the dark. His *Giants in the Earth,* an epic tale that portrayed the triumph as well as the tragedy of American pioneering, proved to be much more than a best-seller and a typical book of the month. This obscure professor at an obscure church college was an instant celebrity, who cast reflected glory not only on his college but on his Norwegian ethnic heritage.

What few knew, unless they read Lincoln Colcord's introduction, was that within his own Norwegian-American world this man already loomed large after two decades of teaching, preaching, and writing. Even more baffling was the fact that this absorbing tale from a state that many readers knew little about, South Dakota, had been written in Norwegian, and yet it read like an original. The most intriguing part of the "story behind the story" was that the author, a man of fifty-one, had spent his first twenty years in a fishing village by the Arctic Circle, had milked cows and pitched manure on a South Dakota farm, and entirely on his own, had won an education and a degree and a professorship at an American college. From this background he carried with him a spark that he had nourished tenderly by incessant practice in writing: essays, letters, poems, short stories, but above all, novels, four of them, all dealing with his fellow immigrants from Norway. What no one could foresee was that Rölvaag would have only four years more in which to enjoy his fame and to cement it by further writing.

I accepted the invitation to contribute a volume on Rölvaag with some reluctance. For one thing, I felt that my primary competence was not in literary criticism and that I might do my old teacher a disservice by trying to write about him. For another, some might be inclined to dismiss my opinions as being biased, in view of my close association with Rölvaag from before he had won national and international fame. When I nevertheless accepted Professor Leif Sjöberg's proposal, it was out of a sense of happy gratitude to the author who had been my personal and professional adviser and had added to my early life the sense of having been in touch with greatness.

My research has included the obvious and obligatory reading or rereading of every scrap of Rölvaag's writing, as well as giving a course on his work at the University of Minnesota in the spring term of 1981. I profited from discussion with my students and from the questions and term papers that issued from the course. The interest of the students reflected the popularity of the "new ethnicity," and in the following a special effort has been made to relate Rölvaag's views to this topic. Many of his views are today echoed by other writers in other groups.

A problem with all Rölvaag criticism is that the critic ought to know Norwegian *and* English; at least I can claim that qualification over many of my predecessors. I can only regret that severe limitations of space inherent in the format have cut short many of the themes broached.

Acknowledgments to all who have assisted will appear below, but one name needs mention here: that of my wife Eva Lund Haugen, whose patient ear has helped shape my prose and whose ministrations have helped sustain my courage.

Einar Haugen

Harvard University

Acknowledgments

Special gratitude is due the custodians and helpers at the Norwegian-American Historical Association Archives at St. Olaf College in Northfield, Minnesota. The Rölvaag Collection containing thousands of items is in the custody of Professor Lloyd Hustvedt, secretary of the association, Miss Charlotte Jacobson, archivist, and Professor Odd Lovoll, editor, all of whom have been most helpful. Also within easy reach in Northfield are the writer's old friends, now retired, Professor Kenneth O. Bjork, former editor, and Professor Clarence A. Clausen, historian (who surely must be Rölvaag's oldest living student and a quintessential Norwegian-American).

The manuscript has been read and criticized by Professor Leif Sjöberg, editor of the Scandinavian Series of Twayne books, and by Ella Valborg Tweet, Rölvaag's daughter. Other members of the Rölvaag family who have helped are Governor Karl F. Rolvaag, Solveig Tweet Zempel, and Torild Tweet Homstad. Others are the librarians and archivists of St. Olaf College; Professor Gerald Thorson of the English department there; the librarians of the Minnesota Historical Society and Luther College; Professor Harold P. Simonson of the University of Washington; Clarence Kilde; Robert Bjerke; and Dr. Ulf Beijbom of Emigrantinstitutet in Växjö, Sweden; Professor Arthur Huseboe of Augustana College, Sioux Falls; Jan Hovey Johnson of Estelline, South Dakota; Øyvind Anker at the Universitetsbibliotek in Oslo; Jon Austad and wife, our hosts at Dönna; and art weaver Else Halling in Oslo.

Anyone who works on Rölvaag is deeply in debt to previous scholars, above all, Theodore Jorgenson, Nora O. Solum, and Gudrun Hovde Gvåle. One feels constantly that one is treading well-worn paths in going over the Rölvaag material. But it has been possible also to make use of later research, including unpublished theses. At all times, however, I have tried to form my own opinions, even while respecting those that differ from mine. There have been some happy finds, for example, the Mimmi Swensen letters, and there are many quotations not previously used in the literature.

OLE EDVART RÖLVAAG

Gratitude is hereby expressed to Harper & Row, Publishers, New York, for permission to quote passages from books by and about Rölvaag, and to Rölvaag's heirs, Ella Valborg Tweet and Karl Fritjof Rolvaag, for letters and other unpublished materials.

Chronology

1876   Ole Edvart Pedersen born April 22 at Rölvaag, Dönna Island, in Helgeland district, County of Nordland, Norway, third child of Ellerine (Ella) Pedersdotter and Peder Benjamin Jakobsen, fisherman.

1891   In January, makes first of six annual fishing expeditions to banks off the Lofoten Islands.

1893   Barely survives fierce storm; considers emigration.

1896   Receives ticket from uncle in South Dakota, decides to use it. Leaves July 29, arriving in New York August 20 and in Elk Point, S.D., via train, August 23. Works on Sivert Eidem's farm for two years.

1898   Matriculates at Augustana Academy, Canton, S.D., in November. Replaces patronymic Pedersen with Rölvaag as family name.

1901   Graduates with honors from Augustana; enrolls at St. Olaf College, Northfield, Minnesota.

1904   Writes first novel, "Nils og Astri" (Nils and Astri); never published.

1905   Graduates with B.A. from St. Olaf College. Borrows money for year of postgraduate study at University of Oslo; enrolls that fall.

1906   Takes equivalent of M.A. degree with grade of *praeceteris* at Oslo; starts teaching at St. Olaf, both in the academy and the college, chiefly Norwegian.

1908   Married at Garretson to Jennie Berdahl of Garretson, S.D., on July 9. Naturalized as an American citizen.

1909   *Ordforklaring,* glossary to Rolfsen's *Second Reader.* Son Olaf Arnljot born June 25.

1910   Daughter Ella Valborg born December 8.

1912   *Amerika-Breve fra P. A. Smevik til Hans Far og Bror i Norge,
       Samlet ved Paal Mörck* (America letters from P. A. Smevik
       to his father and brother in Norway, collected by Paal Mörck),
       a novel. Builds family home at 311 Manitou St., Northfield.

1913   Son Karl Fridtjof (later governor of Minnesota and ambas-
       sador to Iceland) born July 18.

1914   *Paa Glemte Veie* (On forgotten paths), a novel, under pseu-
       donym Paal Mörck.

1915   Son Paul Gunnar born March 2. Son Olaf Arnljot dies Sep-
       tember 22.

1916   Summer visit to Norway, mostly at home on Dönna. Be-
       comes chairman of Department of Norwegian.

1918   *Deklamationsboken* (The declamation book), a reader.

1919   *Norsk Læsebok I* (Norwegian reader, vol. 1), edited for chil-
       dren; includes some of his own poems and stories.

1920   *To Tullinger: Et Billede fra Idag* (Two fools: A portrait of our
       times), a novel. *Norsk Læsebok II* (Norwegian reader, vol.
       2), selections from immigrant authors, including himself.
       Gives first courses in English (Dramas of Ibsen; History of
       Norwegian Immigration). May 18, drowning of son Paul
       Gunnar leads to crisis in his thinking.

1921   *Længselens Baat (The Boat of Longing)*, a novel.

1922   *Omkring Fædrearven* (Concerning the ancestral heritage), book
       of essays. Builds family cottage on Big Island Lake in north
       woods of Minnesota (near Marcell).

1923   Sabbatical year from college to work on novel, which he
       starts at the cottage, but interrupts to help in fund raising
       for college after chapel fire.

1924   Leaves for Norway February 7; finishes novel *I De Dage—
       Fortælling om Norske Nykommere i Amerika* (In those days—:
       A story about Norwegian immigrants in America). Accepted
       by Aschehoug in Oslo, wins wide critical and popular ac-
       claim. Spends six weeks in Nordland; returns for fall se-
       mester in Northfield.

1925   *I De Dage—: Riket Grundlægges* (In those days—: Founding
       of the kingdom). Assists in founding of Norwegian-Amer-
       ican Historical Association; is elected secretary.

1926   King of Norway confers Order of St. Olaf. Contact is made with American writer Lincoln Colcord, who rewrites translation of *I de dage*— and secures publication of book with Harper's.

1927   *Giants in the Earth: A Saga of the Prairie*, a translation combining the two parts of *I de dage*— into one volume. Instant success, Book-of-the-Month Club selection. Rölvaag becomes a celebrity.

1928   *Peder Seier (Peder Victorious)*, a novel.

1929   *Peder Victorious*, translation of the preceding by Nora O. Solum and the author. For reasons of health, winters in Biloxi, Miss. Receives Honorary Litt. D. from University of Wisconsin.

1930   *Pure Gold*, a novel, revision and translation of *To Tullinger* (1920) by Sivert Erdahl and author. Winters in Miami, Fla.

1931   *Den Signede Dag* (The blessed day), a novel, translated as *Their Fathers' God* by Trygve M. Ager. Resigns position at St. Olaf College. Dies of angina pectoris in Northfield, November 5.

Chapter One
Life and Work:
The Uncoiled Hawser

On February 18, 1928, the fifty-two-year-old Ole Edvart Rölvaag was the guest of honor at a dinner hosted by Harper and Brothers at the Players' Club in New York. Among those present were Thomas Wells, editor of *Harper's Magazine*, Harry Hansen, editor of the *New York World*, Samuel Morison, famed historian and Harvard professor, assorted authors like Thornton Wilder, Julia Peterkin, and Fanny Hurst, and of course, his sponsor and cotranslator, Lincoln Colcord. Eugene Saxton, Rölvaag's editor at Harper's, presided, and though he had promised there would be no speeches, he could not resist offering some words of tribute to the new star in Harper's firmament. The year before, they had published *Giants in the Earth*, a novel of Norwegian pioneers in South Dakota, which had become an instant popular and critical success. Saxton then urged Rölvaag to share with them something of his own background.[1]

Rölvaag responded to this unexpected challenge by telling the story of his life from his days as a fisherman just under the Arctic Circle to his struggles as an immigrant in the New World. As he told it in a letter to his wife: "I was in a strange mood. . . . I felt as if I stood in the midst of a great stillness; I suffered a sadness such as I have never felt before; yet I was strangely joyous. And so I told my own story, very slowly and brokenly, picking my words carefully as I pieced together my sentences. Never have I been less eloquent. . . . Here I was standing in the most exclusive club in New York, talking to a rather important group of men; the old Castle Garden, where I first stepped on shore in America, only a short distance away. I saw my whole life in retrospect, clearly as one looks at an uncoiled hawser. . . . This dinner is the highest honor I've had paid me. But never have I understood my own race and its destiny as clearly as when I stood there speaking. . . . The speech was very poor, yet I doubt if any of the men will ever forget it."[2]

The story of his life as Rölvaag told it on that occasion is not preserved for us. But it has been told and retold elsewhere, and in this chapter, we shall recapitulate those features that bear most directly on his work as a writer.[3] In Rölvaag's own fisherman's imagery, we shall follow his uncoiled hawser back to its moorings. His report on the New York impromptu reveals a temperament that swayed from joy to melancholy and from modesty to pride. It also hints at his deep concern over the future of those whom—in the terms of his time—he could call his "race." These were the Norwegian immigrants in America, who constituted that "Norwegian-America" in which most of his work was done. This was a world of its own, a lively and fruitful way station on the immigrants' long journey from Norway to America. We shall probe here his relationship to that world and its significance in his growth as a man and an artist. It is a story that is still largely untold.

Roots and Moorings

Although most of Rölvaag's stories take place in America on the prairies of the Middle West, the thought of his childhood home is never very far away. In the opening chapter of *Giants in the Earth*, Per Hansa with his family and their caravan is pushing his way through the tall prairie grass: "The track that it left behind was like the wake of a boat—except that instead of widening out astern it closed in again."[4] Even after a lifetime of land-locked living, Rölvaag remained at heart a man of the sea, on and by which he had spent the first twenty years of his life.

The fishing hamlet that bears the name Rölvaag faces the North Atlantic from the extreme northwest tip of the island of Dönna.[5] Just above the sixty-sixth degree of latitude, its place on the globe corresponds to that of northern Alaska, Baffin Island, the glaciers of Greenland, and the frozen tundras of Siberia. Thanks to the Gulf Stream, its climate is well suited to human habitation. The island has been described as barren and windswept, but it provides an adequate living for its inhabitants. It is a miniature Norway, with lakes, fields, woods, and mountains; it is large enough to sustain two churches and the Dönnes estate, to which the Rölvaags as crofters owed some small service each year in lieu of rent.[6]

On this spit of land, six generations of his family had farmed and fished when Ole Edvart Pedersen was born April 22, 1876, to Peder Benjamin Jakobsen (1846–1931) and Ellerine (Ella) Pedersdotter (1845–1915), as the third of their eight children. We are tolerably well-informed about Rölvaag's family and childhood. The earliest of his autobiographical accounts is one that he wrote to his fiancée Jennie Berdahl, a Norwegian-American girl from South Dakota, soon after their 1904 engagement. In this he writes: "My parents are and have been poor, hard-working fishing folk. Both father and mother are richly gifted, especially father. He is clever, logical in his thinking, and very humorous. Mother, however, is more reticent than father. She is indeed a rare woman. . . . They are both true Christians."[7]

Rölvaag repeatedly expressed his deep love for his kindly, understanding mother: "I was mother's own boy while I was home." Next to his mother came his older brother Johan: "As soon as I was old enough to handle an oar, I had to go to sea. I and my oldest brother, Johan, were constantly together." They were known far and wide as "the Rölvaag boys," who were said to have no fear of wind or weather: "No wave was too high for us and no storm too strong." He calls himself a "wild one," and tells of how he would remove his cap and "let the storm muss my hair and the rain lash my face."

But the brothers had more in common than their courage: they were both voracious readers. Ole developed his reading ability more slowly, but once he had caught up, they "raced each other at reading." Schooling was minimal, consisting of three three-week sessions annually and terminating at age fourteen, when the children were "confirmed," a Lutheran rite of passage ensuring that they could read and write, and that they knew their catechism and Bible history. But the boys had a better resource: they trudged some seven miles to a local library, where they nourished their hunger for reading with novels, not only by such Norwegian classic writers as Björnson and Lie, but Swedish Tegnér, Finnish Topelius, and Danish Ingemann. There were also translations of foreign classics: Dickens and Scott, Dumas and Goethe. Rölvaag later admitted that Cooper's *The Last of the Mohicans* was the first novel he read. The household, for all its poverty, was a literate home, where books were read aloud in the evening, and two newspapers from Oslo furnished materials for discussion of national and world news.[8]

The home was also a place for telling stories. In his boyhood, all
the lore for which Nordland is renowned was still a living part of
its tradition. A fragment of an autobiography written in the last
year of his life deals mostly with this lore. "All things began and
ended in mystery," he wrote; as the evenings lengthened and dark-
ened toward winter, the people of the house would shorten their
busy tasks by telling stories.[9] "All nature was alive with the super-
natural. In the barn lived the *Nisse*, in the hills the *Good people*, in
the glens and dales the *Hulder*, in the sea the mermaids, the sea-
serpent, and the *Draug*—the most awful of all of them." There is
good reason to think, as Jordahl has suggested, that this vigorous
tradition of storytelling laid the foundation for Rölvaag's own ability
as a narrator. Even when he is at his most realistic, he manages to
give his story a twist of the wonder and mystery in which he first
saw the world.[10]

But the main concern was the livelihood that came out of the
sea. "I can almost say," he wrote to Jennie, "that I spent my entire
childhood in a struggle with the Arctic. This struggle has left an
indelible impression on me; for the passions of my soul are as
powerful as the storms up north." Later he added, "Solitude had a
great attraction for me. I loved to be alone with my intense longings
and dreams of achievement; for I would achieve great things, when
I grew up; of that I was convinced. Once—I recall it as well as if
it were yesterday—mother asked me what I wanted to become.
Without hesitation I answered: either a poet or a professor. You
can just imagine how she laughed; for how could a poor fisherman's
boy ever become anything like that?"[11] There was certainly little
prospect of it, for he was no sooner confirmed in 1890 than he was
packed off for the first of six annual expeditions to the Lofoten
Islands. This jutting archipelago furnished much of the world's
vitamin-rich cod-liver oil as well as the stockfish that was one of
Norway's major export items.

By sail and oar the fishermen from Tröndelag to Finnmark would
make their way by the thousands to these dangerous work sites. In
1893 an unexpected and furious storm without parallel in the annals
of the North came close to destroying the boat and crew with which
Rölvaag shipped. In most accounts of his life, this event is credited
with triggering his decision to emigrate.[12] But in the aforementioned letter to his fiancée, he motivates it quite differently, as we
shall see.

Uprooting and Transplantation

If one visits the site of Rölvaag's birth, as I did in 1980, one can understand, not only why he had to leave it, but also why he never ceased to dream about it. [13] The two-story timbered cottage is still there and inhabited, not much different from what it was in his day; one wonders how it managed to house the eight children who were born there. The stone steps down to the boat landing, worn by many generations, are still there, as are the sea and the mountains that frame men's and women's lives in one of the most dramatic and kaleidoscopic settings one could hope to find. On the island itself is the Dönna Man, a mountain resembling a man lying on his back, with a beaked profile that is easily identified with that of the Norwegian poet-hero Björnson. Beyond that, the eastern horizon is dominated by the Seven Sisters, a chain of towering peaks; to the north is the cone-shaped island of Tomma. Although the sea is open to the west, it is dotted by innumerable islands that make for good fishing and that also in some slight degree protect Dönna from the worst impact of the Atlantic. The weather is no less dramatic: a summer that is all daylight, a winter that is twilight and night.

Rölvaag repeatedly re-created this scene in his writings, most poignantly in the first part of his novel *Boat of Longing*. [14] In writing to his fiancée, he even attributed his restlessness to its influence: "I started early yearning to get 'out beyond the high mountains' " (a phrase from an oft-quoted poem by Björnson). [15] "I believe it was my natural surroundings that created this longing in me; for to me there is no nature in the world so magnificent, so powerful, so bewitching and wonderful as that of Nordland . . . sea and moun-tain, mountain and sea. . . . No doubt the sea . . . created my longing and . . . made me poetic, if that is what I am." From the promontory, he stared out to sea: "It brought me a greeting from the unknown that I longed for." "This longing grew along with my ambition. That I had to become something great in the world was clear to me, and perhaps this was what drove me to leave for America."

"When I was nineteen years old, I saw clearly that I could not possibly stay at home, for there I could never become anything but a fisherman. . . . I had—and still have—an uncle who lives down by Elk Point, South Dakota. I wrote to him, asking for a ticket, which I got, and so I came here in the fall of 1896. I had no desire to come here, no, none whatever. I just felt that I had to. It was sad to leave home, inexpressibly sad, and worst of all was to part from my mother."

This simple account, written to the woman who would become his wife and within eight years of his immigration, differs from some of the accounts put out in later years, but it bears the stamp of an honest confession. He did not leave for economic reasons; after six seasons in Lofoten, he was a fully accomplished seaman and was actually offered the command of his own boat if he had chosen to stay.[16] He was the only one of his seven siblings who did in fact leave, and his favorite brother Johan even regarded it as a kind of treason. Ole left because America, as he knew from his wide reading, could offer opportunities for creative as well as material gain. Today his bust, inscribed in bronze, marks the Nordland rock from which he was hewn.

The decision to leave for America was neither easy nor obvious, and any explanation falls short. But it was not unique, either for Norway or for his region. In that year, nearly seven thousand Norwegians emigrated. Of the more than three quarters of a million who left Norway between 1825 and 1924, Rölvaag was something like the half-millionth emigrant.[17] A whole literature of guides and warnings had sprung up; one novel that we know Rölvaag read was by a Norwegian-American, H. A. Foss.[18] In his *Husmandsgutten* (The crofter's son) of 1884, Foss spun an ever-popular tale of the poor Norwegian boy who earns a fortune in America and returns to win his princess and an estate back home. Rölvaag promised his parents, as had so many emigrants, to return in ten years; he managed to keep his pledge, but then only for a visit. He also promised his puritanical parents that he would never dance or drink, and could assure his fiancée that he had done neither, although he was sorely tempted by one (no doubt the dancing; in Norway he had managed to attend thirteen dances in one Christmas season!).[19]

Rölvaag left Dönna on July 29, 1896 and that evening, made the first entry in his diary, which he sporadically confided in for nearly five years (to January 10, 1901). Naive, often awkwardly phrased, it is nevertheless his first literary work preserved to us.[20] It begins: "So now I have really left. Had I only realized that it would be so hard to leave my mother—and everything else—the girl I love so dearly. I really thought my heart would break, but of course it didn't. Nor did I lose my mind, as I thought for a long time I would." The diary teems with this kind of boyish pathos, mixed with anticlimactic humor, like the remark about his "heartbreak." He tells the story of his journey from his home to the capital Kristiania (now Oslo), where he boarded the steamer *Norge*, arriving in New York August 20. The voyage was no trial for a hardened seaman. The diary is chiefly concerned with homesickness, religious scruples, and affairs of the heart. It reflects his wide reading by numerous quotations; he turns to it "to cheer his heart."

His destination was a farm near Elk Point, South Dakota, three days' train ride from New York, where the uncle who had lent him money for the ticket was employed. On the train Rölvaag discovered that meals were not included, but he spent the one dime he had on a packet of pipe tobacco. Through a misunderstanding, his uncle, Jakob Fredrik Jakobsen, was not at the station to meet him. He got a bite to eat from a passing Swede and then headed out on the prairie to find the Sivert Eidem farm where his uncle worked. That evening he saw his first sunset on the prairie.[21] The beauty may not then have concerned him so much, but he would re-create it unforgettably in his writing.

Rölvaag has also reported these experiences in his first published book, *Amerika-Breve* (discussed in Chapter 3). Looking back on them, he could see their humor; in the diary we see more of the young newcomer's despair. His ambition to "accomplish something" is much on his mind: "I feel that within me there are forces that stir . . . but perhaps they are merely due to the reading of cheap novels. . . . But this is certain, that if I am going to do anything or become anything, it will have to be somewhere else than here in Union County, South Dakota."[22]

In this still pioneering environment, he missed a library above all, though soon he was able to borrow books from the Norwegian pastor, Peter J. Reinertsen. Reinertsen also advised him to go to school, first to Augustana Academy in nearby Canton, South Dakota, and then to St. Olaf College in Northfield, Minnesota. Both of these were English-language schools founded by Norwegian Lutherans, where Norwegian language and literature was also taught and where most of the students came from Norwegian Lutheran homes. Reinertsen's letter of recommendation of his protegé to President Kildahl at St. Olaf is enthusiastic, aside from one detail: "He is a newcomer, has read much (entirely too much) Norwegian literature, history, etc."[23] We detect in this reservation the suspicion in which the clergy held secular literature; Reinertsen of course assumed that Rölvaag was headed for the ministry.

In November 1898, Rölvaag matriculated at Augustana Academy, late, so that he could earn money in the harvest. Having paid back his uncle, he was now free to enroll, but he was also entirely on his own. During academy and college days, he earned his tuition and keep by working around the school, and in the summers, by selling stereopticons and books. As a college student, he could also go out to teach Norwegian and religion in the summer parochial schools maintained by many Norwegian congregations.[24] Aside from modest earnings, he garnered rich experiences for future writing. Here, on the western, newly settled frontiers of Norwegian-America he lived and worked among his own people, observing their foibles and their fortitude, the themes of much of his writing.

The teachers and subjects he encountered at the schools and on the farms were crucial for the realization of his ambitions. He learned English at Augustana, as he might also have done at the University of South Dakota in nearby Vermillion; he might have attended Carleton College in Northfield, as did the famous economist Thorstein Veblen (1857–1929), another Norwegian-American farm boy. What he could not get at these two schools and did get at the Norwegian-American ones was the opportunity to work in and on his native language, Norwegian, and to prepare for a life in the service of his own ethnic and religious group. From his diary and letters, it is evident that this became his life's goal at an early age. On March 14, 1898, he wrote about the countrymen he had met in South Dakota: "There would be a splendid field of work here for one who knew how to take hold of things, a splendid pioneer's job if one could transform these merely *existing* beings called 'people' into *thinking* beings."[25]

His joy in the schoolwork found expression not only in his letters and the diary but also in his grades. In his senior year at St. Olaf College, he made two crucial decisions. One was to become engaged to Jennie Berdahl, whose background and interests were similar to his own and whose well-balanced common sense could offset his own temperamental ups and downs. The other was to plan for a career of teaching rather than of preaching (though he never quite gave up the latter role), and specifically to become a professor of Norwegian language and literature. The college made him a loan for graduate study at the University of Oslo for 1905–6. On his return, he was appointed instructor at the college, which became his forum for the next quarter of a century.

The engagement was followed by marriage in 1908 and the building of a permanent home in 1912 on a newly created street called Manitou (no. 311, now designated a national monument). With these events we can say that the transplantation had taken place: he became an American citizen in 1908, and his roots were firmly replanted in American soil barely a decade after he had stepped ashore at Castle Garden in New York City.

Professor and Poet

Rölvaag had achieved one of the goals he had announced to his mother: becoming a professor. What about the poet? He had not for a moment lost sight of creative writing as his ultimate goal. Much of his classwork in the literary courses consisted of writing inspirational essays for use as speeches or in college debates, poems published in the college paper, the *Manitou Messenger*, and stories, some of which reached print. In 1905, his senior year, he started grappling with his first novel, "Nils og Astri" (Nils and Astri).[26] He was still innocent enough to think that the sale of it would finance a year of study in Norway. But neither then nor later in 1911 when he rewrote it did any publisher find it salable. As the title hints, it is a love story in a rural immigrant setting. The subtitle is "Fragments of Norwegian-American Folk Life."

In spite of its many imperfections, this debut contains many Rölvaagian ideas and characters. Its main problem for the Norwegian reader is its all-too-obvious dependence on Björnson in theme, narrative technique, and style. Only the setting is original, with characters transported to America. Like Björnson's "folk" novels, it belongs to a genre known in Norwegian as *folkelivsskildring* ("tales of folk life"), a regional and rural genre, much like the "farm novel" in America.[27]

The job Rölvaag was hired for was to teach young men and women to read and write their ethnic tongue, which most of them had at least learned to speak in their homes. No one had given him any assignment to write books, least of all secular storybooks that were more literary than edifying. The value of his academic subject was obvious enough to those students who were going out to become pastors in predominantly Norwegian-speaking congregations, of which there were many hundreds by this time. But as the American world within which the immigrants and their children lived intruded more and more on their personal as well as their social and institutional lives, Rölvaag found that students, colleagues, and even leaders of his church were increasingly less willing to invest academic time and money on the "un-American" language and literature of their fathers. Only as long as new immigrants kept coming could one take the teaching of Norwegian for granted. Rölvaag thus found himself in a defensive position. Being a courageous, hard-hitting personality, he carried his teaching off his campus into the Norwegian-American community. He soon found himself the leader of a faction within the ethnic world that argued most ardently for the preservation of old values. He joined and organized societies that held fast to these values, and he lectured and wrote articles to uphold his cause.

We may call this the "preaching" part of his work: Norwegian language and culture became his chief gospel. But how could he still write literature? It is one of those mysteries of personality that he succeeded by sheer willpower in becoming a professor in his college, a preacher-prophet to his people, and to top it off, an author famous and beloved both in Norway and America. He published four novels in America that made him the leading Norwegian-American novelist. He published four more in Norway that made him well-known there and in translation won him a secure position in American literature.

In the following account, we shall consider each of his novels in some detail, but also try to give a broad picture of the man behind the books. His work as a teacher, an ethnic leader, even as a textbook writer are all relevant to his life and personality. They may even be more relevant today than earlier, now that many Americans are actively searching for their roots and take pleasure in the identities they have inherited from their ancestors.

Lincoln Colcord, whose crucial role in bridging the gap between Rölvaag and mainstream America will be recounted below, was deeply impressed not only by Rölvaag's writing but also by his person. He has left us what may be the most vivid account we have of Rölvaag, after their first meeting in Northfield in 1926:

"He is the short, thickset, fighting type, and I can see that he has fought for every inch of his life and his artistic achievement. . . . Whether his work is to be received in English or not, he is entirely confident of its artistic worth. . . . He is simple, direct, and fundamental without a trace of self-consciousness, a man who would compel interest in any gathering. . . . He retains in a rare way the viewpoint of the man with both feet flat on the ground—smokes a cigar to the very butt, swears fluently, and is chiefly interested in the elements of life. At the same time he has acquired much of the college professor, a certain sternness and precision of mind along with his boyishness."[28]

That Rölvaag was an avid smoker, perhaps to his own detriment, is unquestionable, but his swearing was completely under control.[29] Colcord's most significant statement relates to Rölvaag's isolation from American literary circles: "He tells me that never before in his life has he been met on just this ground, or felt himself in touch with the publishing profession in America. Doesn't this seem incredible? He simply has had no contacts. Such is the lot of the alien in our midst."[30]

What neither Colcord nor anyone else who met Rölvaag could suspect was that this man who seemed to manage every task that was laid upon him and to reach every goal he had set himself was under sentence of death.

This vigorous man with the boyish temperament and the hearty laugh had suffered more than one bout with illness. Much of his year's study in Oslo in 1905–6 was upset by illness. He had attacks of pleurisy that made him suspect tuberculosis, the chief scourge of Norwegian communities in his youth. The real enemy was his heart, which kept him inactive (or as inactive as the doctors could persuade him to be) during much of 1926. His intense love of life may have been fostered by awareness of its potential brevity. He knew that he might have only a short time to enjoy the fame that came to him, and he worked to the very end, which came on November 9, 1931. Earlier that year he had written to a woman in Oslo, whom he had met at the Ibsen centennial in 1928: "I think it is very charming of you, madam, to remember me. . . . My heart is worse, so help me! It is an ailment that has a beautiful, resonant, classical name—angina pectoris. I am proud of the name, but the illness is bad. It requires of me that I live 'a quiet, godly life, free of all sin.' And a person who can't sin now and then is surely to be pitied! But I do not complain. One has to take life as it comes."[31]

As a worthy son of the Vikings, he could meet even death with a jest. To his brother Andreas in Norway he wrote: "I have never been much afraid of death. Many of my own people have trod the path ahead of me. Hell I have never believed seriously in, at least not in a hell after death. And if there is a better place, I shall meet several there whom I on this earth have loved more dearly than any word can express."[32]

At age fifty-five, the hawser of his life snapped and broke.

Chapter Two

The Arsenal of Textbooks: "High on Manitou Heights"

St. Olaf College in Northfield, Minnesota, is a Lutheran school named after a Catholic saint: the common denominator is that both were Norwegian. Founded in 1874 by immigrant Norwegian churchmen, it is today a prosperous, forward-looking liberal arts college, one of the strongest and most respected Lutheran-affiliated schools in the United States. While covering the usual range of college subjects, it marks its historical identity by maintaining a Department of Religion and a Department of Norwegian Language and Literature. In this way it honors doubly the martyr king who by his death in 1030 secured the foundation of Christianity and nationhood in Norway.[1]

The Department of Norwegian was not created by Rölvaag, but for a quarter of a century, it was his living, his platform, and his daily concern. Without the training that he got and gave in this department, his mastery of the Norwegian language and his literary achievement in that language are quite unthinkable. He had told his mother he wanted to become either a poet or a professor. As it turned out, he became both, but the teaching was the means that made his creative writing possible. It enabled him to overcome his late start, his humble, dialect-speaking background, and his miscellaneous, unsystematic reading. He admitted in later life that authorship was his ultimate goal,[2] but he never stinted his teaching. He threw himself into this work with all his life. Only after he was assured of literary success and threatened by ill health did he throw off his teaching and resign from St. Olaf. But then it was too late to recover the time and energy he had given to his students.

St. Olaf: "Fram, Fram, Kristmenn, Krossmenn!"

The college that bears in its seal King Olaf's battle cry ("Forward, Forward, Christ's men, Cross men"), with the appropriately dem-

13

ocratic omission of "King's men," was founded as "St. Olaf's School" by Norwegian-born Reverend B. J. Muus.[3] Under the presidency of another pastor, the Reverend T. J. Mohn, it promoted itself to a college in 1889. Without the sponsorship of an organized church body, however, it pursued an uncertain course amid rumors of being tainted by "the spirit of humanism," as Rölvaag once ironically put it.[4] But survival, along with religious orthodoxy, was assured when, in 1899, the college was adopted by the United Norwegian Lutheran Church. Installed as its new president was the Reverend John Nathan Kildahl (1857–1920), who in 1906 would appoint the young Rölvaag to its faculty.

Kildahl's inauguration signaled a new era. The United Church, dating only from 1890, was a middle-of-the-road synod, comprising congregations that rejected both the high-church, German-oriented "Norwegian Synod" and the low-church, pietistic "Hauge's Synod."[5] The Norwegian Synod maintained Luther College at Decorah, Iowa, and the Hauge's Synod had a college at Red Wing, Minnesota. The United Church was destined to grow and eventually absorb, or better, be united with its chief rivals in 1917 under the comprehensive name of the Norwegian Lutheran Church in America. By this time St. Olaf had become the largest college among the Norwegian immigrants, and its Department of Norwegian a focus for Norwegian activity far beyond the confines of the campus. Rölvaag became chairman in 1916, succeeding his teacher and colleague, P. J. Eikeland (1852–1927).

Much of the inspiration behind Rölvaag's choice of a lifework can be traced back to his two teachers of Norwegian, the Reverend J. S. Nordgaard at Augustana (1852–1925) and Eikeland at St. Olaf. Later he would refer to them jointly as "my two dear teachers" who "awakened my interest."[6] These, in turn, had sat at the feet of Professor Thrond Bothne (1835–1907) at Luther College and "heard his rousing words." "He awakened their spirits to such a degree that they had to go back to Norway and study further. Then they came back and became teachers among our people."[7] Bothne has been described as "an intellectual giant" who was one of the "brightest names" in Norwegian-American academic and journalistic life.[8]

What Nordgaard and Eikeland transmitted to their gifted student was a characteristically Norwegian enthusiasm for the harmonization of religious and nationalistic commitment.[9] Nordgaard was a native of Gausdal, Norway, where the Reverend Christopher Bruun had established one of the two first folk high schools of Norway (1867). Bruun, a model for Ibsen's relentless Brand in the play by that name, embodied the either-or ideas of the Dane Kierkegaard in a framework developed by the more genial Grundtvig.[10] Eikeland has been described as a "religious humanist" who "virtually lived and moved and had his being in the Bible and in Norwegian literature."[11] In his memorial to Eikeland, Rölvaag wrote, "Nothing much would have come of me if it had not been for him."[12] In 1910 the three of them met at a conference in Minneapolis and spent their Sunday on a feast of reminiscences at Minnehaha Falls Park. In a letter to his wife, Rölvaag reported, "Each of us drank eight glasses of buttermilk that day!"[13] The buttermilk can stand as a symbol of the nonalcoholic but jolly mood of the occasion. These men had in common a cause to which they had committed themselves: the teaching of their native language and its literature at a church school with whose religious foundations they were in substantial harmony.

St. Olaf College calls itself "the college on the hill," towering as it does on Manitou Heights and overlooking the beautiful rolling prairie of Minnesota, as well as the still bucolic town of Northfield. When President Kildahl entered office, all activities, plus his own living quarters, were centered in Main Hall, now known as Old Main. Today a peaceful classroom building, it was then (in Rölvaag's words) a "Noah's ark," even housing "a bunch of unruly boys who were supposed to gain knowledge and culture."[14] The only other building was Ladies' Hall, a modest dormitory for the young women who attended this coeducational school. By 1906, when Rölvaag started teaching, there was also a men's dormitory, a library, a power plant, and a chapel. By 1919 the academy section had been removed, and the 48 college students of 1899 had grown to 550, taught by some thirty-five faculty members. This was the period when the American college population was outgrowing the general population four to one. The burgeoning prosperity of the Norwegian settlers of the Middle West encouraged and enabled them to send their children to college, preferably one of their own church schools.

Even with its new status, the college offered its faculty more scenery than salary. In Rölvaag's second year of teaching, he was earning only $650 plus room and board. As he assured his fiancée, this would be enough to get married on.[15] She agreed, and Rölvaag entered upon the career that to him was not just another job but a life mission.[16]

The problems a young teacher of Norwegian faced could seem formidable enough. To a fellow Nordlander, the Reverend O. C. Farseth, he confided in 1908: "When I think of my position here at St. Olaf, I would rather sail a small craft from Fleinvær to Værö [in Lofoten] on a stormy January night and be responsible for boat and crew alike. Once upon a time I knew how to sail, and that without fear and trembling. But to guide so many young people? I have to stop every now and then and ask myself, 'Is this the right course? Am I steerin' straight, I wonder?' "[17]

In a newspaper article of 1911, Rölvaag expounded the problems of Norwegian as a subject in American schools: lack of textbooks, trained teachers, and interested pupils.[18] In a vivid passage, he described the classroom situation: "Side by side with the immigrant, who can speak his dialect with vim and vigor, but has no technical knowledge of standard Norwegian (*Rigsmaal*), sits the American boy, stammering in his broken Norwegian-American. Obviously the latter will have a harder time of it than the former. . . . The teacher has to keep things going as best he knows how. Many a class hour toils its weary way like a number on an old, worn-out music box: now and then you hear a pure note, then one that is virtually inaudible, then an ear-splitting disharmony, then a hobbling sentence, then one that splits in the middle, then one in a totally foreign tongue."[19]

This article is Rölvaag's first salvo in his lifelong war on behalf of the ancestral tongue.

Textbooks and Teaching

In the early years, most classroom texts could simply be ordered from Norway, and most students had a foundation of knowledge from their parochial school training. Eikeland had published a grammar in 1908, but written as it was in Norwegian, it could be used only by advanced students.[20] It fell to one of his students and later colleagues, J. A. Holvik, to write the texts that were for many years a mainstay of college-level teaching.[21] In these, the explanations and the glossaries are in English.

Rölvaag was also enlisted in this enterprise, and his first published book was a glossary to be used with volume 2 of a popular school reader by Nordahl Rolfsen, for many years the standard text in Norwegian schools.[22] The glossary (1909) was actually bilingual, supplying both Norwegian synonyms and English glosses for each word. This work, trying as it must have been to his patience, may also have taught him a good deal about both languages. In spite of an occasional error, his mastery of English was already quite good. He even started on a Norwegian-English dictionary, which was badly needed, but he was happy as a lark when he learned that someone else had assumed the task.[23]

His next textbook was produced in collaboration with Eikeland, a handbook in Norwegian orthography and pronunciation (1916).[24] This little volume was needed for those who wished to stay abreast of developments in Norway. A radical reform of the spelling had been officially adopted in 1907, the first break with the Danish spelling that had also been Norwegian since the Middle Ages. It represented a first step, after the political independence attained in 1905, toward linguistic autonomy. Rölvaag and other teachers of Norwegian welcomed it and adopted it in their textbooks and other writings. Publishers of Norwegian-American newspapers, fearing the loss of older subscribers, clung to the old. All of Rölvaag's own books would appear in this new dress, even after a second reform in 1917, still more radically different from Danish and closer to Norwegian speech. He did not live to see the most radical change in 1938; only in the most recent editions in Norway have his books been revised into this current form, which by its more vivid rendition of speech suits his books very well.[25]

The textbooks that gave Rölvaag the greatest satisfaction, however, were the readers by means of which he hoped to keep alive student interest in the treasures of Norwegian literature.

The first of these was *Deklamationsboken* (1918), so-called because its selections were to be declaimed at contests organized for young learners. The selections were picked, he wrote, for their modest length and high interest to young people. The poems, folktales, and short stories are not all by literary giants, but are generally both entertaining and edifying. Among the short stories are three of his own, previously published.

In the succeeding years of 1919, 1920, and 1925 appeared three further volumes, edited jointly by Rölvaag and Eikeland, under the title *Norsk Læsebok* (Norwegian reader), volumes one to three. We shall here pass over volume three, a history of Norway and Norwegian literature, primarily by Eikeland.

These volumes were modeled on the previously mentioned readers by Rolfsen, but with suitable adaptation to Norwegian-American conditions. Along with Norwegian classics, volume 1 includes several items by Rölvaag himself. Some are new, like a charming story about a rabbit called "Langøre" (Long Ears), a poem "Bluff og Prairie" (he did not hesitate to introduce English words commonly used in Norwegian-American speech), and an essay on "Why we must attend religious [i.e., Norwegian parochial] school."

Volume 2, for high school students, was the real heart of the series for Rölvaag. It is written entirely by and about Norwegians in America. He intended it to be an inspirational book for the people (folkebok), and he noted that his chief problem had been "the lack of good material."[26] "Those of us who have tried to write have been inspired by melancholy, pathos, grief, or sorrow; or else by indignation and anger. Very few have tried to idealize the really great and good things we have accomplished since we became Americans." "It is a task very dear to my heart to make the younger generation understand that we Americans of Norwegian stock are well descended, that we have done great deeds since we came, that we have created something that is really our own." In spite of this ideological bias, it is no doubt the best anthology of Norwegian-American writing. Of his own writing (for which he apologized), he included a poem and a story previously published and two passages from his novels. His new contributions are all programmatic and historical.

These three volumes, handsomely illustrated and printed in Minneapolis by Augsburg, the church publishing house, are a monument to Rölvaag's (and Eikeland's) work in the vineyard of Norwegian textbook making. They came in the eleventh hour, but are no less admirable for that. Especially in the second volume we see Rölvaag the author at work, gathering the bricks for the literary mansions he dreamt of creating.

In 1927 Rölvaag reminisced about the St. Olaf he had met as a freshman in 1901: it was a patriarchal, restrictive community with only two prescribed course plans to choose from. Fixed study hours were required morning, noon, and night: "Doors bolted tight and all lights out at 10. No student using tobacco was allowed quarters in the dormitory; smoking on the streets or on the campus absolutely forbidden, with a death penalty for cigarette smoking."[27] The jesting tone masks the fact that as a young teacher Rölvaag approved of restrictions that limited the outside activities of students. As resident head of the men's dormitory, he earned the resentment of the students he had to discipline. He wrote to Jennie that he half expected a strike and that he had lost much sleep over the matter.[28] He was also critical of the students' one-sided concern with future economic success, which drew them away from "tedious intellectual work" to the frills of college life. Yet he confesses to having had "a glorious time" as a student, and as a teacher, rejoicing every time a new building was added: "We felt we were part owners in the concern on Manitou Heights."[29] Over the years, he wrote many a news story in the Norwegian-American press effectively telling about St. Olaf.[30]

His unswerving loyalty to St. Olaf did not preclude his vigorous criticism; if anything, it required that he speak out more forcefully. As the school grew and its students were increasingly recruited among second- and third-generation Norwegian-Americans, the college took on the coloration of what one president called "the standard American ideal college."[31] Mohn, its first president, jestingly wrote to a Boston acquaintance that he headed "an institution founded by Norsemen for the purpose of turning Norwegians into Americans."[32] They needed only to look across the Cannon River to find on the other side of Northfield a model for such an American college, Carleton. Founded (1866) by New Englanders of Congregational persuasion, it provided for the immigrant Norwegians an ever-present (and not always beloved) standard of comparison with their own achievement. Yet there was always a difference: St. Olaf yielded slowly and reluctantly to an Americanization that threatened religious values. It was not a segregation on the order of the Amish or the Mormons; but the special fusion of Lutheranism and Norwegianism was a powerful factor of selection in the early years. Mohn had declared at the dedication of Main Hall in 1874, "This religion the Norwegians ought to retain in their hearts, cherish in their schools, and bring, with their other treasures to the common altar of our adopted nation."[33]

Rölvaag took seriously the idea of American enrichment, but as the appointed guardian of the "other treasures" of the Norwegian heritage, he was bound to suffer many disappointments. Religious liberty was written into the American Constitution, but there was no provision for linguistic or cultural liberty. To be an American was to speak English. Freedom of speech did not embrace support of non-English languages and cultures.[34]

Rölvaag's commitment to his cultural-religious ideals characterized his teaching of Norwegian literature. His lectern was his pulpit. As one student has put it: "He entered the classroom with a firm step and with the manner of one on a mission. There is work to be done here." "Rölvaag's lectures were not just information and interpretation, . . . but also enthusiasm. . . . . There were such very important considerations as standards in morality, loyalty to family and cultural ancestors, and disciplined standards of work."[35] I can testify, from one semester of classes with Rölvaag, that this characterization is correct. Rölvaag saw in his students the bearers of his own mission, to whom he wished to impart some of his enthusiasm. He took endless pains with the work of his students, giving them time (according to his daughter Ella) that his children sometimes begrudged.[36] The student cited above, who took his courses in the rebellious late twenties, tells of being called to Rölvaag's home to discuss a paper of his. "At first Rölvaag explained to me how ridiculous I was. This got my hackles up. Then he commended me on some things I had said, and I was so humbled I wanted to crawl under the rug. Now he became jovial, as he rose to terminate the conference. At the open front door he had the last word, 'Clarence, I predict the day will come when you will honor your ancestors.' "[37]

Rölvaag's alternation between severity and facetiousness, seriousness and jollity, was an important aspect of his temperament. Students crowded into his classes, especially after 1920 when he initiated two courses in English: one on Ibsen's plays, another on Norwegian immigration.

The College on the Hill

As a member of the faculty, Rölvaag could be a thorn in the flesh, to both his colleagues and the administration. The two presidents under whom he served most of his time, Kildahl and Lars W. Boe, were poles apart: Kildahl the great preacher and man of God, Boe the administrator and academic politician.[38] Yet both were Rölvaag's friends, the former as his spiritual adviser, the latter as his contemporary whom he could counsel on the future of the college and his work there.

In his early years Rölvaag could write despondently to Farseth: "At bottom the cause of my depression is this that my work here seems to be fruitless. I might as well haul manure. If nothing else, it would at least stink. I can see scarcely any difference between St. Olaf College and any other Protestant American college. What then do I have to do here? If we have no special mission, why do we try to exist at all?"[39]

Rölvaag's more positive assessment is found in letters he addressed to his two chiefs. The one to Kildahl was written in 1918, after Kildahl had left to become a professor of theology at the seminary in St. Paul; but it was to be sent only if Rölvaag failed to recover from an appendicitis operation he underwent.[40] It is a spiritual testament to "my people." He calls for better understanding by the church people of the work of their schools, which might lead to livable salaries for the teachers and an appreciation of the importance of the Norwegian heritage as a contribution to American life. "The work that I have done in the interest of Norwegian culture must be the work of the entire institution." Of his own work he writes, "I have tried with all my might to lift our youth to higher visions, to inspire and to ennoble them."

Besides a stiff requirement of three years in religion courses, the college maintained a one-year requirement in Norwegian for all students which was modified in 1923 to "students of Norwegian ancestry"; by 1930, it could be replaced by "a course in Norwegian culture."[41] In his letter of resignation of 1931, Rölvaag wrote to Boe: "The Norwegian Department at St. Olaf College has always fought an up-hill fight. . . . I am tired of the struggle, and so I get up and get out."[42] He expresses bitterness at the attitude of jealous colleagues to the privileges given his department. "One of your doctors of philosophy had the effrontery to ask me what I intended to do with all the teachers in Norwegian. To which I answered candidly, 'We'll shoot them!' and then I walked away because I was too angered to speak to the man decently. . . . I have slept many an unslept night over the problems of the Norwegian Department at St. Olaf College."

Perhaps the greatest test of his devotion and loyalty to the college came in 1923, when he interrupted his first sabbatical to solicit funds for the college after the chapel had burned. To a concerned friend, he wrote: "There is scarcely anyone in the world who sees more clearly than I what this school can be both for our people and

our heritage, what a glorious monument St. Olaf College can become
to the Norwegian immigrant."[43] From mid-November to Christmas, he laid aside his masterpiece, the book that became *Giants in
the Earth*, to travel around raising funds for rebuilding. Happily he
was still able to complete his writing and win the fame that re-
dounded in great measure to the honor of his college.

In 1944, thirteen years after his death, the college honored him
and itself by dedicating its stately new library to his memory and
naming it the Rölvaag Memorial Library.[44]

Chapter Three
Letters from America:
The Ethnic Imperative

In Rölvaag's day, the term *ethnic* was not yet applied to American immigrant or racial groups, and the term *ethnicity* had not even been invented. Like *sibling*, it began as a bit of sociological jargon that became popular because it filled a hole in the English language.[1] Before the 1950s, such words as *nationality* or *race* had been used. But a term was needed that would neither emphasize biological differences, like *race*, nor suggest conflicting political allegiance, like *nationality*, and that would not be pejorative.

Now that the term has become widely known and used, it seems fitting to apply it to the concerns that were central to much of Rölvaag's thinking and teaching. In the *Harvard Encyclopedia of American Ethnic Groups* (1980), the Norwegians in the United States are included and are given an article of their own.[2] Since the term also applies elsewhere in the world, and not necessarily to immigrants, it is not easy to give an unambiguous definition. As good as any, but still inadequate, is Joseph Hraba's: "A self-conscious collectivity of people, who on the basis of a common origin or a separate subculture, maintain a distinction between themselves and outsiders."[3] This reflects the dual characteristics of ethnicity: it must have a common core of positive content and a set of formal limitations that constitute its borders: inward inclusion, outward exclusion.

However vague the term, it can usefully be projected backward to Rölvaag's thinking. When he spoke of his "people" (*vårt folk*) or his "kin" (*vår ætt*), he meant his ethnic group in America, and when he spoke of its "ancestral heritage" (*fædrearven*), he meant its Norwegian "ethnicity." To him the preservation of that ethnicity as intact as possible and its infusion into the developing American culture was an ethical duty laid down by divine fiat in every ethnic group. It was implied by the commandment to "honor thy father and thy mother that thy days may be long upon the land." This is why we may call it an "ethnic imperative."[4]

We shall now review his first published novel, *Amerika-Breve* (Letters from America, 1912) and see how he embodied this idea in the story.[5]

The Three Lives of Per Smevik

A Norwegian immigrant named Paal Mörck, not otherwise identified, lives in a mythical Clarkfield, South Dakota, where he has made friends with an elderly Norwegian named Smevik. His son, the Reverend P. A. Smevik, is known as a "gifted and zealous servant of the Lord," but Mörck finds the father "one of the most unusual personalities" he has known. Mörck learns that Smevik has kept the letters that son Per had written home after his departure for America. He persuades the Smeviks to let him publish these because of their general interest, and the result is a book of "America letters from P. A. Smevik to his father and brother in Norway," allegedly collected by Paal Mörck.[6]

The twenty-three letters run from August 26, 1896, shortly after Per's arrival in Clarkfield, to July 29, 1901, in Lewisville, North Dakota, where Per is teaching summer school after graduation from the academy. He has won the signal honor of being chosen as one of the commencement speakers at the academy.

The early letters reflect the newcomer's jumble of bewildered impressions of the new land, yielding gradually to a more mature and resigned acceptance. The book is thematically rounded off by his mother's death and the decision of his father and brother to follow Per across the sea. He begs them to say a special farewell from him at his mother's grave: "And when you see the coast of Norway sinking into the sea, will you whisper a goodbye from me then, too. I don't imagine I'll ever be doing so myself" (184).[7]

In the first letter, he comments that he feels as if he has already lived three lives on earth: his first, the twenty years in Smevik, his second, the three weeks of travel to Clarkfield (already like an eternity), and third, the life he has just begun: "God alone knows how long the third life will be and how long it will seem" (11).

Although this "third life" is the main theme, we are given many glimpses of the first and second as well. He often refers to life back home and eagerly asks for news of recent happenings. We learn that he had spent his life fishing in northern Norway and that his home is on an island off the coast. He complains about the chores he is set to do on a South Dakota dirt farm, unaccustomed as he is to life inland so far from the sea. A line of verse that they used to hum in their boat recurs to him as a kind of motif in the letters: "Rolls the billow, so broad and bright, from shore to shore."[8] He misses his beautiful Nordland and the jolly occasions when he and his friends got together in simple enjoyment of nature and song. He has lost much of what he took for granted at home.

Language is of course a first hurdle. Even in his uncle's household, where they speak Norwegian, the old dialect is only half comprehensible. His uncle calls him down to "brækfæst" instead of "frokost" and serves the food, prepared in "ståven" instead of "omnen," on a "pleit," not on a "tallerken." His uncle baffles him completely when he gives him "svillpeilen" instead of "søppelbytten" and tells him to "slabbe pigsa" with it when he means to "gi grisene." He is embarrassed also to be doing "woman's work," such as milking, and begs his brother not to breathe it to his friends back home. These predominantly minor and amusing experiences point a contrast between his new and his old life.

Per also reports in some detail on his "second" life, the journey from north to south in Norway, then from the capital, Kristiania, to New York, and by train to South Dakota. His limited, rural background is reflected in his amazement at such cities as Trondheim and Kristiania, not to speak of New York and Chicago. In Kristiania, he sees an art museum for the first time in his life, and in his rural innocence he is embarrassed by the array of nude statues: "To tell the truth, I can't say I found it very edifying" (36). When the shores of Norway sink beneath the horizon, he goes below to his cabin and "cries like a child who's been spanked. That was my farewell to my fatherland" (37). The description of Per Smevik's journey to the Promised Land tallies closely with Rölvaag's own, as we have sketched it in Chapter 1.[9]

Per Smevik's America

The America that Per reflects in his reports back home is that of a well-established immigrant farming community at the turn of the century. Its older members had been pioneers in the 1870s, Norwegian immigrants who came from the land and went to the land.

Their children were now grown and bilingual, often preferring to speak English among themselves. Per feels left out and starts on the long path of acquiring the language. He reports with comic despair on some of his problems with this funny language, in which he could not hear the difference between "pens" and "pants" and no doubt said "pance" for both (65).

The America that he experiences, first on the farm, then at the academy where he enrolls in his third year, is pictured in a series of dramatic episodes. Most of them are humorous, told as comic illustrations of his helplessness or as pointed vignettes of life among his countrymen. He finds women churchgoers "shamelessly over-dressed" but pale and wan as if they had never "smelled of the Lord's blessed sun and rain and wind" (42). He earns undreamt-of wages, but has to slave hard through long, hot days. He tells of making friends with an Irishman on the thrashing crew, but also of having to put down a crosspatch of a fellow Norwegian by main force (55–56). He can impress the others by his seamanship in repairing a block and tackle, but only after nearly getting killed in a quarrel between two neighbors. The immigrants are shown as endowed with a variety of quirks, some good and some bad.

In the spring of 1898, the Spanish-American War breaks out, and just to get away from the farm and back on the sea, Per decides to enlist in the navy. But his employer pleads with him to stay for the harvest, and after that he enrolls instead at the Norwegian-American Academy, "if only to learn English" (106). As with his life on the farm, Per reports his own creditable as well as comical experiences, for example, how he crams English grammar to catch up with the class after registering late. He is determined that by examination time he will be at the head of his class. To earn his keep, he works at anything available, including a try at selling a church history to Norwegian-American farmers. One prospect turns him down by telling him that he knows pastors too well to want to read about them; another says that they don't have time to read books; a third offers him "honest" work on his farm; and a fourth lectures him on what a terrible school he is attending, which causes Per to lose his temper (it turns out that the man's nephew had been dismissed for misbehaving).

Life at the academy is Per's joy, for now he has at last a chance to read books and use his brains. He enjoys the democratic spirit of the school as demonstrated by teachers as well as students. But he also feels a lack of something which he tries to formulate as the "resonance" that a good fiddle should have. His teacher in Norwegian has phrased it as "enthusiasm for the great ideals of life," "the deep, compulsive longing that each rightminded youth should feel for the inexpressible" (136). As he looks around at his fellow students, he senses a lack of materials for leadership. "There are few kingly skulls here" (135).

When he goes out to the local congregations to teach parochial school, he observes even more disquieting phenomena. Many congregations are rent by doctrinal disputes, with such tragicomic effects as husband and wife joining different congregations. In his work as a parochial school teacher, he is embarrassed to be called on for such pastoral services as an occasional sermon or a funeral. In one poverty-stricken home, he finds an atheistic father and a believing mother paralyzed over the dead body of their child, miserable instances of the potential tragedies of immigration. Here the father denies and the mother affirms that the child is baptized; we are reminded of Beret and Susie in *Their Fathers' God*.

On the night Per's mother in Norway dies, he dreams that she comes to visit him. When he learns that she is in fact gone, he feels as if a secret place in his heart, a room that contained all that was beautiful and memorable in life, is locked up forever. She symbolizes for him all that his mother country had meant to him.

It is therefore fitting that he should consider at this point what he has gained and what he has lost by emigrating. He does so under the guise of copying out a Fourth of July speech by a Norwegian-American, as a way of advising his father and brother on what they may expect.

The unnamed speaker reminds his listeners that most of them are only "adopted children" of this country. America is therefore "our land, not our fatherland." He then asks exactly what they as emigrants had "gained and what we lost" by exchanging "our fatherland for our land." One by one he lists the gains: prosperity, ambitiousness, intellectual growth, civil and religious liberty, unlimited opportunities. But the costs have also been stupendous, and not just in the hard work and the deprivations endured.

First of all was the loss of the ennobling and educative influence of a grand and powerful nature. Then there was the loss of a fatherland: "We have become strangers. Strangers among the people we left and strangers to the people we have joined" (171). After developing this theme, the speaker admits that it is impossible to express in words what was lost: "We lost the inexpressible." This carries over into the second and third generation, and no one knows how soon the loss will be overcome.

The speaker enlivens his address with an anecdote about a gipsy tinker who is asked to remove a waltz tune from a music box and replace it with a hymn tune. The dubious result is that the box now plays "a hymn melody in waltz time," with snatches of both in alternation. "So it is with us foreign-born in this country: we are neither the one nor the other. We are both at the same time" (173).

Who Is Per Smevik?

It will not have escaped the attentive reader that Per Smevik is a thin disguise for Ole Rölvaag, that Clarkfield is Elk Point, and that the unnamed academy is Augustana. The times of arrival and graduation coincide virtually to the day. Contrary to the diary, there is nothing here about his religious problems or his love affairs. Many of the episodes can be confirmed as Rölvaag's actual experiences; others may be. His mother's death did not occur until 1915, and the emigration of his father and brother never occurred at all. Per chose the ministry, which Rölvaag rejected in favor of teaching. These unbiographical features serve to round off the story artistically and lead up to his peroration. His brother suggested that Ole only needed to copy out his own letters, but even if he had copies of them, it is improbable that they served as more than raw material. We cannot know, in any event, since they were lost or destroyed (reportedly from fear of tubercular contagion). [10]

However autobiographical, the Per of these letters lives as a free artistic creation. The cheerful and enterprising Per is certainly one aspect of Rölvaag's character. We meet a quite different aspect in the apprehensive, brooding young man of the diary from the same years. From the diary to the letters, there is also an immense leap forward in literary quality. The overall purport of the book is beyond the horizon of a raw immigrant. This is made clear by the other two spokesmen Rölvaag has provided for himself.

The anonymous Fourth of July speaker is of course Rölvaag, who had given this very speech at Winger, Minnesota, on July 4, 1911. As Paal Mörck, he takes us by the hand in the preface to tell us what the book is about: the acculturation of the immigrant. The name Mörck is a plausible family name, but can also be taken as the word *mörk*, meaning "dark." Rölvaag once declared that he had adopted it to shield the privacy of his family letters.[11] But he would continue to use it for literary purposes until 1916 (including his second novel). The idea of a double pseudonym was right at hand in Kierkegaard's *Either-Or*, in which an editor Victor Eremita publishes papers by writers A and B "found" in an old writing desk.[12]

The Winger speech had gone through various metamorphoses, as detailed by Jorgenson and Solum.[13] The idea of the value of one's native heritage was developed in his commencement speech at Augustana in 1901. Under the title of "True Culture on a National Foundation" (Sand dannelse paa national grund), which, according to the only known account, was the best oration of the day, he "laid down three conditions to the acquirement of true culture, viz., a Mother Tongue, National Characteristics, and the Faith of the Forefathers."[14] Without the Mother Tongue, "one loses his nationality and becomes a sort of international vagrant, belonging nowhere." In a Fourth of July speech of 1903 in Lime Grove, Nebraska, he used the word play on "land" and "fatherland," which does not make for smooth translation, since in English one would prefer *country* for *land*.[15]

The theme of the ethnic heritage, including "Mother Tongue, National Characteristics, and the Faith of the Forefathers," was one that Rölvaag would never tire of proclaiming, whether in his teaching, his textbooks, essays, lectures, or his fiction. We shall therefore have to return to it from time to time. As Rölvaag presents it in his writings down to 1912, the emphasis is on the spiritual and cultural homelessness of the immigrant. *Materially* he has found a new and better home, but he is no longer "part of a harmonious whole," or able to "feel patriotic fervor." "In short, we have become rootless. . . . We are quite simply outsiders" (171). It would be hard to find a more eloquent statement of the condition of *marginality*, a term first launched by the sociologist Robert Park in 1928 and explored by the Swedish-descended Everett Stonequist in 1937.[16] Neil Eckstein has shown how the "marginal man," who is poised between two worlds, may have a keener eye for the weaknesses of both.[17] Among Norwegians, he exemplifies this with the writer H. H. Boyesen, who joined the WASP establishment, Thorstein Veblen, who spent his life as an outsider and critic, and Rölvaag, who "sought to strengthen the Out-WASP's own world, to build, as it were, a third world of immigrant culture in order that the uprooted might strike down roots, the stranger might join with other strangers and find a new kinship."[18]

Rölvaag could do this because he came at a time when Norwegian-America, which had been flowing westward with the frontier, was flourishing as never before. With its hundreds of churches and publications, its pastors and writers, still for the most part working within the structure of Norwegian Lutheranism, it was a whole little world of its own. But he also came right on the heels of Frederick Jackson Turner's declaration in 1893 that the frontier was closed.[19] With that Norwegians had nowhere else to go but into urban America with its intensive industrial and capitalistic growth, a twentieth-century America that rejected the rural values of thrift and simplicity in favor of "conspicuous consumption." As Harold P. Simonson has shown, the closing of the frontier also meant the symbolic end of the American dream of unlimited expansion. "Instead of a limitless frontier there is a wall."[20] Rölvaag saw the handwriting on that wall, and he set himself to consolidate the ethnicity of his countrymen so that their identity would not be crushed against the wall. From his marginal role, he rose to become the great mediator and bridge builder.

Epistolary Art

The epistolary form was suggested to Rölvaag by a now forgotten novel, which caused him to say to his wife, "If I couldn't do better than that, I wouldn't even try."[21] The form is of course as old as the novel itself: we think of Samuel Richardson's epoch-making *Pamela* (1740) and *Clarissa* (1748). Travelers' books about America were often cast in letter form, from the Frenchman Crèvecoeur's *Letters of an American Farmer* (1782) to the Swedish Fredrika Bremer's *Homes of the New World* (1853).

If *Amerika-Breve* is a novel at all, it comes close to the format of a *Bildungsroman* à la *Wilhelm Meisters Lehrjahre* (1796) by Goethe. The form is defined by Burgess as being "about the processes by which a sensitive soul discovers its identity and its role in the big world."[22] Per Smevik grows from naiveté to maturity in the New World and finds himself a place within it. The climax comes when he tears himself loose from parental domination and goes off to school. The style is carefully differentiated according to recipient: with his father he is more formal and distant, with his brother, more spontaneous and humorous. (One wonders why he never addresses a letter to his mother in view of his frequently expressed love for her; can she be thought of as illiterate?) The language is enlivened from time to time by dialect words that express intimacy and, as time goes on, English words that reflect a growing distance.

If not a masterpiece, it is respectable and can still be enjoyed for its vignettes of immigrant farm life and its portrayal of the Americanization of a bright, if naive immigrant youth. Most readers are likely to find that the overly lengthy Fourth of July speech, however eloquent, is a static passage. Here the author steps into the action and preaches over the head of his hero.

Arrangements for publication in Norway regrettably fell through, so that it was available primarily only to his emigrated countrymen. It was well received by reviewers in Norwegian-American journals: "We can recognize ourselves in these well-written letters . . . straightforward and lively . . . he could well have used his real name, since he has no reason to be ashamed . . . an original idea . . . an interesting and well-written book . . . lively and humorous . . . it deserves an eminent place in our Norwegian-American literature."[23] Most of these are by pastors, whose encomiums might be expected. The most penetrating review was by Kristian Prestgard, an editor of *Decorah-Posten*, himself an outstanding writer: "This story has enriched our impoverished Norwegian-American literature by one more good book."[24] He compares it to Jacob Riis's much-read *The Making of an American* (1901): "After a while we begin to think that we are ourselves Per Smevik and that we have written these letters with our own hand. . . . These problems are admirably suited to the epistolary form." "And in this case we continually have a pleasant feeling that behind the 23-year-old writer there stands a mature, experienced, and judicious gentleman, who whispers good and wise words and remarks in his ear."[25] Without knowing who the anonymous author is, Prestgard hopes that one may hear from him again.

The most interesting and to Rölvaag surely the most meaningful review was one that never reached the public, but was written by one of the models of its characters, his older brother Johan, known in the book as Andreas. Although ailing (he would die later that year), Johan wrote an eighteen-page account of his pleasant shock upon finding himself in a book and offered penetrating comments. He notes that his brother has avoided the chief danger of the epistolary form, monotonous repetition, and that he has developed a terse style, learned from Björnson and reminiscent of the sagas. He enjoys the humor and would have liked even more. But its real greatness, he believes, lies in the "vibrant undercurrent" of his love for the homeland. He urges his brother to write more about the beauty of his birthplace and to become for his countrymen in America "a prophet who can come among them and with his mighty inspiration tear them out of their earthbound existence."[26]

It might seem necessary in view of the disheartening sales: his countrymen bought 471 copies in the course of its first four months, yielding a royalty of $47.10![27]

Chapter Four
On Forgotten Paths:
Faith of the Fathers

Rölvaag's second published novel, *Paa Glemte Veie* (1914), in his most neglected in the critical literature, in part because it has never appeared in English.[1] But in Rölvaag's own development as a novelist, it is an important milepost. Contrary to "the easiest possible task" (as his brother Johan put it) that he had set himself in *Amerika-Breve*, he now tackled the problem of creating a plot with plausible characters and a significant message. He returned to the scene of his earlier book, but now reached down into deeper layers of immigrant psychology. Against a background of rural Norwegian South Dakota, he created a story exploring the interplay of love and religion, themes that were conspicuously absent in *Amerika-Breve*. Per Smevik tried to explain to his relatives the religious conditions among his countrymen, but dwelt mostly on the controversies and their disastrous effect. This time he hit upon themes that point forward very clearly to *Giants in the Earth*.

As noted earlier, Rölvaag's diary of 1896 to 1901 gives us a very different picture of the young immigrant than does *Amerika-Breve*. What he confided to his diary included deeply personal experiences that he clearly would not care to display in his letters home. For one thing it reflects his religious turmoil. Leaving as he had a home where religion was an ever-present part of life, he prays to God for protection.[2] After a visit to the Trondheim Cathedral and a Salvation Army meeting, he piously hopes "that God in His great mercy will count me as one of His children for the sake of Jesus Christ."[3]

His attempts to gain clarity on whether he was indeed a child of God were sustained by a series of encounters with young women. On the boat, he discussed with a "spiritually kindred" girl from Telemark "the life of the soul and its development."[4] In South Dakota, his spiritual life was guided by "the most perfect woman

33

I have met to this day."[5] But when he did feel that he had become a "child of God," it was the work of another woman with "secure, childlike faith," who, alas, got herself engaged to someone else, leaving him to feel "like a man innocently condemned to death."[6] Pastor Reinertsen advised Kildahl at St. Olaf that Rölvaag had "experienced a religious awakening."[7] To his fiancée Jennie, he emphasized the importance of being "a child of God."[8] His plans for their family life included grace at every meal, Scripture reading at breakfast, church every Sunday: "I am a crank on that."[9] He became a loyal member of St. John's Congregation, was its secretary for some years, and a member in good standing to the end of his days.

The result was a novel, weaving together the love of God and the love of woman on behalf of the "Faith of the Forefathers."[10]

Forgotten Paths

"Chris Larsen was the richest farmer in the whole Clarkfield settlement." With this promising first sentence Rölvaag (still disguised as Paal Mörck) brings us back to the South Dakota settlement that received Per Smevik (alias Ole Rölvaag) in 1896. Chris was one who came early enough (probably in the 1870s) so that he could grab great allotments of land and quickly expand his original homestead. His success, however, was flawed by the unhappy temperament of his wife, Magdalena. To this brooding soul, emigration was "the great sin of her life." Her nostalgia has "caused her longing for Norway and her longing for heaven to flow together." Norway is heaven, while "everything that was cold and evil belonged to the prairie."[11] "There was nothing to hide behind" (37).

In this conflict between husband and wife, it is not hard to see foreshadowed that of Per Hansa and Beret in *Giants*. Here, too, the prairie rears its ugly head for the first time in the role of a "troll," man's spiritual adversary whom the pioneer must overcome. Otherwise, the novels are very different, not only in development, but also in their tone and skill of presentation. There are typical Rölvaag touches of humor and psychological insight, but we still have a long way to go before this torso is fleshed out.

Chris wants a son and is disappointed when the first child is a girl. The mother wants to name her Magdalena Marie, but Chris insists that she must have a "real prairie name," and calls her Mabel.

The wife "could not understand how any child could grow up with such a name, far less get into heaven" (11). The second child is indeed a boy, but he dies in an accident within a month. The father is so distressed that after he has buried the child in a grave dug on the farm, "he mumbles harshly" to the heavens above: "Well, after this I'll try to manage by myself. You won't need to concern Yourself with my affairs again!" (13).

But this is only the first of the trials that the Lord visits upon Chris Larsen. After some years, when Mabel is adolescent, mother Magdalena is carried away by the spring floods and drowned. Chris decides to start afresh at the new frontier in Alberta, where there is still pioneering to do. He gives Mabel a chance to stay in Clark-field, but she decides that her father needs her and joins him on the bleak and still untouched prairie of Canada.

So far the introduction. From here the story becomes a conflict between Mabel and Satan for Chris Larsen's soul. The *via dolorosa* that she has entered is the struggle to win her father for God. The novel is structured into three parts: "the path that was hard to choose," "the path that was hard to follow," and "the last hill."

Chris is in his element on the still untamed prairie. He is rejuvenated when facing the same tasks as twenty years earlier: "The prairie was just as endless as the heavens that swam above him. And when he interrupted his breaking of the land and leaned against the plow while the horses took a breather, when he looked the length of the fresh furrow of rich, brown-black topsoil, on which the sun glittered, then his whole body tingled in well-being. In his mind's eye he saw before him the world's greatest foodbasket. . . . He snarled like a hunting dog with its forepaws on its prey" (35).

But again Chris is visited by calamity. One day he is crippled for life by an accident with a team of runaway horses. Mabel takes over the running of the farm and proves to be a capable manager. But her mother had brought her up to be more concerned with the hereafter than the present. After a mystic experience of contact with the divine, she becomes a child of God: "She got hold of God's hand, touched it timidly, and then was able to put her own securely in his" (36). It gradually dawns on her that her father, who now demands her constant care, is not only an unbeliever but a blasphemer. In her unhappiness, she is reassured by a dream vision of her mother, who tells her, "Now you will get your father back;

just take good care of him." From this time on, it becomes her "call," her mission in life, to bring him to God (50).

It is indeed a hard path to choose, for cantankerous Chris is not about to be converted. All his unrepentant thoughts are of the prairie, which he blames for all his troubles and in whose evil he believes just as firmly as Mabel believes in the goodness of God. The prairie "was to him like a huge troll that brooded over fabulous treasures and the ineffable happiness of life. . . . To wring these from it by his own ingenuity and the strength of his hands had been his life's great passion" (55).

But now his pride has been humbled or rather frustrated: "A huge fist had suddenly been thrust out of the universe and had knocked him down, had miserably mutilated him, while the prairie— it was still out there, strong and big and rich as always; no, a thousand times richer now that he had lost his hold on it. Here he lay in his log cabin, a broken straw, a crushed insect, for all the world to jeer at! When his weary thoughts began wrestling with these similes, he seemed to hear the plaintive sighs of the prairie in the winter night changing tune and turning into a taunting, snickering sneer at him and his whole life. 'Now you got it, Larsen! Now you got it! Now you can lie there and twiddle your thumbs. It's no more than you deserved! Now you got it! N-o-o-w y-o-u got it!' " (56).

Chris takes his frustration out on Mabel, whose Christlike patience is sorely tried on this path that she has chosen for herself. From time to time even she falls from grace by losing her temper over her father's perversity. She takes recourse in prayer, and her resolve is strengthened by the visit of a Scottish minister who drops in on them in their prairie cabin.

The second section opens after the passage of some years and in a new setting: Mabel has succeeded in moving her father back to Clarkfield to a more homelike atmosphere. Here we meet their kindly neighbors, the Oplands. Nils, the husband, is an impractical and improvident inventor, who shortly falls ill of tuberculosis and dies. Mrs. Opland watches over Chris when Mabel has to leave the house. But Chris remains obdurate, scoffing at her admonitions: they "stood on different sides of God."

Johnny Opland, some six or seven years old, affords comic relief. Not understanding the gravity of his father's illness, he plies Mabel with questions about when Jesus in his fine buggy will come to fetch the father. Mabel fosters the boy for a time after Opland's death, and he prays with her in his childlike, refreshing way. Once he suggests that if God is coming anyway, he might as well also bring the pony Johnny has been praying for. Touched, Mabel promises him not only one of her own ponies, but a buggy to go with it (280).

Realizing how totally dependent he is on Mabel and secretly admiring her abilities, Chris is now possessed by suspicion and fear of every young man who might wish to marry her and take her away from him. He fixes his eye on the young student pastor, Harry Haugland, who comes to teach parochial school. But Harry is hardly her type, as the phrase goes. While Mabel is struggling "to get closer to God," Harry is an ardent advocate of "social service." He organizes a young people's society, more social than spiritual: "For them all that mattered was to keep having something to do, so they could get together." A motion to donate fifty dollars to the mission is defeated after a long debate that brings out the family rivalries of the members.

Mabel, who does not usually attend, is present and astounds everyone by getting up and tongue-lashing the members for their prattle about "social service," which does not include a sacrifice to spread the kingdom of God. She also contravenes their practice by speaking Norwegian and shames them for not maintaining the bond with their heritage. When Harry later returns as pastor to the congregation, he again shocks her by the lack of spirituality in his ministrations.

By contrast Rölvaag introduces "old pastor Skjærve" who visits the congregation on behalf of the home mission. He is a man after Mabel's heart, who preaches in Norwegian and pictures the sad fate of the thousands of their countrymen who are being lost to morality and religion in the cities of America. Mabel is stirred to think of becoming a missionary herself, but she realizes that her personal call is still to save her father's soul.

After Mabel assures Chris that she is not interested in Harry, he turns his suspicions on a hired hand. In a comic scene Chris offers him two thousand dollars if he will return to Norway. The young man laughingly accepts the check and turns it over to Mabel, who is incensed at her father's machinations. She bitterly returns his check: "Here is your Judas money. . . . These are the pennies with which you wanted to buy me back into slavery." As she looks back on her life, she sees her work as wholly futile, a "fumbling in the dark" (202).

A new minister, young and unmarried, has come to the congregation. He has sacrificed a career as a physician to minister to human souls. He is outspoken and uncompromising: he has chosen the ministry because "he realized that the physical ills of the people were minor compared to their spiritual ones" (211). He is clearly modeled on Ibsen's Brand, behind whom we glimpse Kierkegaard and his attacks on the pastors of the state church. Here Chris's suspicions are more to the point, for between him and Mabel there is an immediate meeting of souls. They could sustain each other's spirituality, just as Rölvaag had experienced it in the love affairs reported in his diary.

Gossip quickly arises over his frequent visits to the Larsens, and Chris becomes aware of their attachment. He accuses his daughter of planning to desert him. She realizes that she cannot accept the happiness offered her until she has won the battle for her father's soul. She tells the pastor that she cannot marry him until her mission is accomplished. A series of unhappy scenes make the pastor decide to leave the community. Meanwhile, one of Larsen's nefarious schemes leads to his being alone when a fire breaks out in his room. He is safely evacuated, but the shock is too much. Before he dies, he asks Mabel to pray for him and begs her forgiveness. Her last act is to write to her pastor friend, who now can hope for the bliss of her company.

The Norwegian Lutheran Heritage

This tale can be read as an exegesis on what Rölvaag meant in 1901 when he listed the "Faith of the Forefathers" as the third and climactic aspect of his ethnic heritage.[12] In spite of his overall loyalty to the church and its institutions, he clearly did not equate mere membership with faith. Lutheranism was (and is) a house of many mansions. Thanks to its status in each European country as a state church, it became more ethnic in America than most other immigrant churches. As Rölvaag knew it, its spiritual jurisdiction was coequal with the political boundaries of Norway. Every Norwegian who did not expressly and formally repudiate it was a member from birth. In the schools, which originally had little other purpose than to train readers of the Bible, religion was still an important subject, and education was considered complete when, at the beginning of puberty, the young man or woman was properly confirmed in the faith.[13]

Although the church could thus reinforce a separatist nationalism and thereby encourage national unity, from the middle of the nineteenth century it had given up trying to enforce total religious conformity. The confession adopted at Augsburg in Germany, Latinized as "Augustana," was the common charter of all Lutheran churches, but without leading to union across national lines. For as long as the ethnic groups of northern Europe remained distinct in America, they were therefore going to set up churches that were ethnic in ritual and spiritual content. But the common ethnicity was far from representing any unified theological outlook. In the state churches of Europe were housed a great store of conflicting views, which in America could and usually did result in lengthy and bitter doctrinal disputes as well as in the establishment of different churches on both the local and national levels (where they came to be called synods).[14]

What had been one religion in Norway thus turned into a *smörgåsbord* of Lutheran synods, large and small, in America. We need not consider the factors of social class, local tradition, or psychological stance that led to individual choices and organizational membership. Suffice it to say that there was among Norwegians a strong strain of lay evangelism associated with the name of Hans Nielsen Hauge, a strain that Rölvaag stood very near. This exhibited an "inwardness" which emphasized personal faith and conversion, a mystic experience of God, often leading to condemnation not only of all "worldly" delights but also of the "dead" faith of their fellow members. In its extreme form, it could cause the condemnation by lay preachers of their ordained brethren, thereby reversing the situation in the early 1800s, when laymen like Hauge were quite simply thrown in jail.[15]

Two other names that were influential in the Norwegian religious scene, without ever achieving the status of Hauge, were the Danish leaders N. F. S. Grundtvig (1783–1872), founder of the Folk High School,[16] and Sören Kierkegaard (1813–55), philosopher of the absolute ideal.[17] In Norway, ideas from both were fused in the life and work of Christopher Bruun (1839–1920), whose book *Folkelige Grundtanker* (1872) was a strong influence on Rölvaag.[18] He met some of the same thinking in Ibsen's play *Brand* (1866). It is generally recognized that Brand's motto of "All or Nothing" is closely connected with Kierkegaard's "Either-Or." The central feature of this peculiarly Scandinavian religious asceticism is its emphasis on the irrevocable choice, just such a choice as Mabel is faced with time and again, when she is tempted to stray from the "call" that has become her mission in life.

Rölvaag's adherence to these ideas has been explored by Harold P. Simonson in a profound study of "Rölvaag and Kierkegaard."[19] We have already seen how they were infused into his teaching at St. Olaf, and we shall meet them again in connection with *Giants in the Earth*. Suffice it to say that *Paa Glemte Veie* is Rölvaag's attempt to portray a life in which these uncompromising ideas are put into practice on the South Dakota prairies. That the attempt was a literary failure is less important than the fact that it was tried. It is one of the consolations of those who hold these ideals that the effort is more important than the success, since in fact success is by definition impossible. Of Brand's motto, Rölvaag wrote in his lecture notes: "I have nothing but good to say of it. . . . It is in perfect harmony with the teachings of Christ."[20] This meant that it was at odds with the usual American conceptions of religion: hence the satire on Harry, the pastor who believes in "social service," and the young people who give up their Norwegian heritage.

Art and Religion

Unfortunately Rölvaag still lacked the skill to create a literary fusion of faith and art, which few if any moderns have managed since Kierkegaard. Large parts of this book sound like a Christian tract. Mabel, who presumably represents Rölvaag's ideal, is priggish and opinionated. Her father, the frustrated pioneer, is more humanly understandable, interesting in all his perverted and almost comical attempts to keep Mabel enslaved. The major problem is of course that a Kierkegaardian attempt to portray the struggle of God and Satan in the human soul (in this case Mabel's, since Chris struggles only in his dying moments) can lead only to a tragic conclusion. Kierkegaard rejected Hegel's notion of synthesis of opposites, leaving no alternative but death, as in Ibsen's play. But Rölvaag provides his Mabel with a deus ex machina who not only permits her to lay down her cross but foreshadows a life of happiness in marriage. As in any good Christian tract, what started out to be tragedy, is capped by a sentimental conclusion.

What most critics have overlooked is the close relation of this book to Björnson's novel *Paa Guds Veie* (On the paths of God, 1889). One can say that Rölvaag here provided an orthodox Lutheran counterblast to Björnson's humanistic story. Björnson, who by this period of his life had rejected the teachings of the church in favor of an optimistic evolutionary humanism, tells the story of two boyhood friends, one of whom becomes a minister, the other a physician. The physician rejects the minister's supernaturalism, and in the end his medical science saves the life of the minister's son. He does this in the face of un-Christian condemnation by the pastor, who finally has to admit that "where good men walk, there are the paths of God." Rölvaag counters that "the paths of God" are those of the church and that they are on the way to being forgotten by the immigrants and their children.

There is more than the title and the theme to remind the reader of Björnson. As his brother Johan had intimated about *Amerika-Breve*, Rölvaag had learned his prose primarily from that writer. Here it is almost painfully obvious, expressing itself in many of Björnson's typical mannerisms. It is striking that as late as 1914 Rölvaag still showed no trace of the neo-romantic style of a Knut Hamsun, whose breakthrough in *Hunger* (1890) had created a new literary epoch. At that time this was still "decadent" to Rölvaag.

The clerical critics of *Paa Glemte Veie* were not surprisingly even more enthusiastic about this book than the first. Only one of them, J. O. Hougen, noticed the parallel to Björnson's book, even pointing out that the name of a major figure is identical: Kristen Larsen vs. Chris Larson. He rightly observed that Rölvaag could get poetry out of even the prairie, which seemed to be "Paal Mörck's paradise and world of fantasy."[21] Rölvaag's chief, President Kildahl, pointed to Little Johnny as his masterpiece, and declared that it is "heartwarming for a cultured Christian to get a book that is truly artistic in form, and in its content is heartening and inspiring."[22] A theological professor expressed his joy at "picking up a book that stands fully on a grounding of Christian faith and frankly confesses its Christian view of life." But he was also aware that the book suffered from great artistic weaknesses: it could easily have been cut by a fourth, and the language is wordy and uneven.[23] Others reject this criticism.[24] In general one can say that the reception was favorable.

As would occur with *Giants*, critics were divided on whether the self-sacrificing woman or the unregenerate man is the central figure.

The leading writer of the day, Waldemar Ager, found the book "mercilessly orthodox."[25] He had little sympathy for Mabel's agony about her father's salvation, and in an essay on Rölvaag many years later, he would observe that Rölvaag never convinced the reader that Chris Larson had any soul left to save.[26]

Yet this book established Rölvaag's reputation and enabled him to abandon his pseudonymous modesty. It was his first attempt to create an original plot with believable characters. The serious theme was enlivened by a degree of playfulness and humor. He would never again attempt to combine art and religion in so obvious a way, and his intellectual development would one day lead him to agree with Björnson's aphorism: "Where good people walk, there are the paths of God."

Chapter Five

Two Fools and Their Gold

Six years were to pass between the appearance of *Paa Glemte Veie* and Rölvaag's next novel, *To Tullinger*, which we shall here refer to either by this title or its literal translation, "Two Fools."

These were years of hard work, but also of sore travail and maturation. In his fortieth year, he became chairman of the Norwegian Department, and in the following year the United States entered World War I. Ever since 1914, a growing agitation for American entry on the side of England had whipped up antagonism to the use of German in the large and powerful German-American community. This antagonism reached its climax with the American declaration of war in 1917 and grew in intensity, not dying down until around 1920, two years after the war.[1]

We have seen how Rölvaag ever since 1909 had been building an arsenal of textbooks to sustain Norwegian teaching. In the years that followed, he carried his campaign for the ethnic heritage to the whole Norwegian-American community by his activity in organizations, his articles, and his speeches. In 1909 he helped organize Nordlandslaget, a society of his countrymen from Nordland; he became president in 1918 and was active in its meetings. In 1910 he was elected secretary of a Society for Norwegian Language and Culture, and in 1919 he became the prime mover and secretary of a society, For the Ancestral Heritage (*For Fædrearven*), with close ties to the church.[2] Under pressure of wartime agitation, the newly united Norwegian Lutheran Church in America decided at its biennial meeting in 1918 to drop the *Norwegian* from its name. Rölvaag engaged himself ardently in opposition to this move, still to be confirmed at a later biennial meeting.[3] Partly thanks to his vigorous articles in churchly as well as secular papers, and partly due to the calmer national temper, the meeting of 1920 reversed the decision, and *Norwegian* was retained until another world war, being finally dropped in 1946.[4]

Rölvaag would call this period "the day of the great beast" in his next book. The utmost border was reached when the governor of Iowa, where many Norwegians were settled, proclaimed that all public use of any foreign language would be forbidden.[5] In Rölvaag's words: "Everything that is not of Anglo-American origin has been rendered suspect to an ominous degree. . . . In some places ill will and suspicion turned into the most rancorous persecution. . . . All that was strange was dangerous; so it had to be extirpated. They were not particular about the means, and woe to anyone who tried to object!"[6] In this controversy he had many of the leaders of his church against him, including his former chief, President Kildahl.

In addition to his disillusionment with the cautious and even negative views of his church friends came the personal tragedies within his own family. His favorite brother Johan died in 1913, his mother in 1915; his oldest son died in the same year, six years old; and his youngest in 1920 by drowning, five years old.

The book that gave vent to his accumulated bitterness and despondency was "Two Fools"; but it also proved to be the best he had so far written, with a tense plot and an entirely new concentration that fell on his Norwegian-American world like a bombshell.

"Two Fools"

The opening section, titled "The Days of the Honeymoon," is full of zest and promise.[7] In the days of horse-drawn thrashing rigs, a large thrashing crew brought life and commotion with it, as well as the satisfaction of reaping a good harvest. Mrs. Öien and their only child, Lizzie, are busy preparing the meal. Lizzie, who flits "light as a lark" from pantry to stove to table, is a young woman in her late twenties. She stops from time to time to cast an eye on Lars Houglum, part owner of the rig, a blond giant of a man just past thirty.

When Lars comes to the porch to wash up, Lizzie playfully splashes him with water. He grabs her, she resists, and before she can escape, he ducks her in the water to the plaudits of household and crew. The suggestive banter they have to endure cements a bond, which leads to their engagement. It is clear even in these lighthearted scenes that her interest in him is more calculating than amorous. She is quick-witted and ambitious, and balances the fact that he is empty-handed and "not very bright at books" against his strength and hard-working habits.

Her ambitousness is reflected in her change of the Norwegian name Lisbet Marie to Lizzie, as she was encouraged to do by the American schoolteacher who pontificated that "it was a barbaric practice for parents to saddle a child with a name that would harm its life."[8] America was a free country; people could call themselves whatever they wished. Now she takes Lars in hand and gets him to change to the "much nicer" American "Louis." So they enter matrimony under the names of Louis and Lizzie Houglum.

They dig in for the usual struggle of young couples to get on their feet economically. With her father's help, they secure a good farm and work doggedly to pay off the mortgage. Lizzie not only takes care of the house but, whenever possible, works in the fields to save the expense of a hired man.

Then a disturbing note enters. One day Louis brings home a ten-dollar gold piece as part of the money received for his harvest. This coin of "pure gold" exerts a mystic fascination on them: "Its soft, yellow sheen glowed so mysteriously toward her, with a light that was gentle and strong at the same time. And the glow varied as she turned it. It was as if it concealed a thousand secrets. She never tired of studying it" (27).

Somehow the young couple's dreams of happiness come to be focused on this gold. Louis suggests that they keep it hidden in the house, as something secure "that no assessor can come and collect taxes on." Their passion for security soon turns their American dream into a nightmare. When it appears that they are not going to have children, the coins they accumulate begin to take their place. When Lizzie fondles the coin, "her strong features grew softer. Finer, as it were. Her large face was filled with something that seemed so good and gentle—almost like when she used to come to him in the first days after the wedding and demand that he kiss her" (28).

It is symbolic that they conceal the coins under the conjugal bed. One night she musingly tries to calculate the dollar value of the full moon! As the years pass, they develop a private language, calling the gold coins "children," the bills "kids," and the silver dollars "money." They take them out in the evening and play games with them: "Within their hefty plumpness lay happiness itself dreaming and dozing away" (57).

But their security is short-lived: a neighbor's house burns, consuming six hundred dollars in paper money. So they deposit their cash—not, of course, the gold—in a bank. Predictably, the bank fails, which, in the days before government deposit insurance, was an ever-present menace. Louis and Lizzie hie themselves to the bank, confident that if only the doors could be unlocked, the authorities would walk in and get their money out. In a masterful scene, they plod from lawyer to sheriff to pastor, in vain, as Louis swears and Lizzie breaks into hysterical tears.

From now on, their money stays on the farm. But society has invented other ways of parting them from their gold. The local Norwegian Lutheran church duns them periodically for support, but with little success. Henceforth they virtually barricade themselves against the world, except for buying and selling, at which they are hard dealers.

Their very avariciousness and isolation make them vulnerable to sharp practices. A salesman representing the "Arizona Pure Gold Company" wins their confidence by saying grace in Norwegian, dressing in semiclerical garb, and behaving in a solemn and sententious way. Although Louis resists through a sort of wariness, Lizzie buys a thousand-dollar share after a campaign of flattery and soft sell awakens her greed. The agent is baffled by her pointed queries: "There was something powerful, something ominous in her—a hidden well of force that he could not recall having met in anyone else" (103). Still she falls, and when the inevitable truth is revealed, she takes to her bed and stays there for a week.

From here on, the action is all downhill. Louis and Lizzie drift apart; she serves such penny-pinching meals that he starts drinking milk straight from the milking bucket. He also withholds sums from his sales and hits upon the idea of carrying his fortune in bills on his body, hidden in a belt made of old canvas. The small bills become large ones. The tellers who do the changing hold the bills up: "Gosh, what a stink!" Another asks, "Did you dig them right out of the manure pile?" In the end, they are each carrying $35,000 on their persons, and Louis carries another $2,000 he has gradually stolen from his wife.

It is 1917 and the United States has entered the war. The Houglums are unconcerned: they have only one value scale, and as their fortune grows, they can't see why people are so mad at "Kaiser Bill." But as time goes on, the war brings a new threat to their savings: the Red Cross and the YMCA join with the government and its Liberty Loan drives to make demands on them. They are assessed for $600 in bonds, and when they refuse to give more than half, the solicitor gets the rest from Lizzie's father.

When these resistances are noised about the community, a more sinister note is struck. Hazel Knap (shortened from the "impossibly clumsy" Knapperud) is a young, busy organizer of Americanism drives. She, as the author a bit obviously describes her, is so full of "git" and "pep" that the "war to end all wars . . . became to her a kind of sacrament that filled her soul." Her fiancé is in France, and from him she can report on all the German "atrocities." She regards anyone who sees the war differently as "unspeakable foreigners and pro-Germans" (161–62).

She stirs up the young men (who are idly waiting for the draft) to go out and teach the Houglums "what it means to be an American these days!" They go out to "scare the liver out of 'em" and "make 'em kiss the flag!" After liquoring up sufficiently, they arrive only to find no one home. Lizzie and Louis have hid in the barn and observe the proceedings through a crack in the siding. The young men are careless with matches while searching the house, and to their dismay, it burns down. No one is ever prosecuted for the crime, but Louis and Lizzie collect the insurance and move into their hen house.

High land prices tempt the Houglums to sell their land and move into town. They soon find that town living is expensive as well as boring: here they have no friends, whereas on the farm "life itself kicked and scratched, grew and sprouted!" One day Louis overhears an Adventist announcing that the end of the world is near. Since this prediction has also appeared in *Skandinaven*, a Norwegian newspaper which is his supreme authority, he goes to his pastor for confirmation. But the minister won't speak Norwegian and doesn't subscribe to the paper, since he opposes "perpetuating a foreign press in America." When the pastor realizes who Louis is, he scolds him for his "disloyalty." Louis goes off pondering what kind of a Norwegian minister it is who won't talk Norwegian: indeed, the end of the world must be near!

Louis has private reasons for worrying about the coming Day of Judgment, since his conscience is beginning to bother him about the money he has stolen from his wife. He drops in on a Methodist service where a hell-fire preacher denounces greed in terms that probably express the author's views on the matter. Louis, who misses his horses, decides to go out to the old farm for a last reunion before the end. It is a stormy day in winter, and he makes his way back to their apartment with difficulty, dying on the stairway. Inside, his wife, thinking it is a robber, has locked the door, and in her penury has kept the apartment unheated. So they both die on opposite sides of the same door. The doctor orders their clothes burnt, just in case they had influenza, and the coroner burns them. "The belts took longer. But little by little the fire devoured them as well" (240).

Toward a Reading

Rölvaag himself reported that he got the idea for this novel from a news item he read about a man digging a basement.[9] He unearthed a crock of gold containing $4,000 and then one with $2,000. "Then the man became frantic, almost mad, because he was sure there was more treasure in this piece of ground." Rölvaag was struck by the "utter insanity" of anyone who could find pleasure in "saving up good money for no better purpose than digging it down into the cold ground." He began building up a picture of a couple who became Louis and Lizzie. Their fate illustrated Rölvaag's thesis: this is what happens "to an individual who has no tradition and no cultural background—we have plenty of them in America!"[10]

Of the two, Louis is the one who has retained some of the tradition: he speaks Norwegian, wishes to read *Skandinaven*, and refuses (like his author) to give up smoking. Lizzie could be compared to some of Ibsen's women, say, Brand's mother, who dies unshriven rather than give up her property. Ibsen's Hedda Gabler can be explained by the fact that she lacks anything to live for; Lizzie blames her own avarice on her father's refusal to send her to business school.[11]

It is significant that this book appeared in the same year as Sinclair Lewis's *Main Street*, the scene of which is also Minnesota. "Two Fools" is a Norwegian-American satire in a vein not unlike Lewis's. The latter's scorn of the dull pretentiousness of small-town America is matched by Rölvaag's evocation of miserliness in the Norwegian-American rural population. In their society, all values are reckoned in gold. But this couple goes to the extreme of saving gold for its own sake, not for anything they could display or enjoy; on the contrary, they wish to appear as impoverished as possible. They are sore beset by the society that surrounds them; money is the key to everything, including the church and its representatives. The American dream becomes a negation of traditional freedoms. Their security is threatened by dishonest bankers, hypocritical swindlers, and a warmongering, repressive government. Mob law operates to detach them from even the shallow roots they have struck in American soil.

The story moves briskly from episode to episode without digressive descriptions or discussions. The dialogue is spare and lively, with much humor. Its realism is enhanced by the author's liberal use of Americanized Norwegian, drawn from his own experience of immigrant speech.[12] When Lars manhandles Lizzie in the opening scene, the farmhands suggest that they ought to *runne ham ind*, "run him in," and when Lizzie responds to his attentions, Lars says, *"Du foola vel ikke, Lizzie?"* "You're not fooling, are you, Lizzie?" Some of the early reviewers found his use of American-Norwegian trying.[13]

Rölvaag's use of "mixed" language was a significant part of his deliberate realism. In a letter to Colcord, he called his style here "the starkest realism. . . . It is, in fact, a fearful thing for one who doesn't see the idealism back of it all."[14] The attack on greed has been, of course, a favorite theme of idealists. One thinks of Jesus' parable of the man who buried his one talent in the ground. In the Middle Ages it was considered one of the seven deadly sins. Molière made it the subject of his famous comedy, *L'Avare* (1688), in which the comic teeters on the edge of tragedy.

Perhaps the greatest weakness of *To Tullinger*, among many good qualities, is the lack of any character with whom we can identify. Louis is weak and stupid, and Lizzie becomes so predictable that one turns from her in disgust. As a psychopathic case, she is more petty than powerful. It is hard to conceive a Medea or a Hedda Gabler in Greenfield, Minnesota.

The book was widely and eagerly reviewed. Ager declared that it was "a significant book . . . interesting and entertaining, which will make a strong and lasting impression."[15] But he also called it "a humoresque that is not funny, a tragedy, whose tragic conclusion arouses loathing and horror, but hardly sympathy. . . . The character analysis is developed, but not well enough to be convincing." He found that the characters were in fact sick, and that the strength of the book was in "the logical development of the disease. . . . The author plays with these two fools like a cat with two little mice . . . finally cracking their necks when they no longer amuse him."

Simon Johnson, another author, called it the best Norwegian-American book of the year, "of such high quality that it will be a milestone in his life."[16] "It has all the marks of a notable author: choice of topic, composition, balance in style and narrative. . . . It is so genuine, so intensely conceived, so honestly executed that it should be received with sincere joy."

Theological professor E. Kr. Johnsen praised it to the skies: "Rölvaag has proved himself as a writer. The book towers high above any other stories written in Norwegian in this country."[17]

There were dissonances as well: some felt that Rölvaag had shamed his own people by implying that they were unusually greedy. One spoke of "an insult to Norwegian immigrants," another wished that he had used his time for something more useful.[18] Rölvaag was defended, and of course no one could fault him for lack of enthusiasm for his Norwegian countrymen. But the book does reflect Rölvaag's idealistic view: for all its realism, it is a kind of sermon.

Pure Gold

After Rölvaag had made a name for himself in the English-speaking world with *Giants* and its sequel *Peder Victorious*, he was eager that his earlier novels should also be known. He retitled the book *Pure Gold*, all reviewers having agreed that *To Tullinger* was a poor title. The title stems from Louis's announcement to Lizzie of his first gold coin: "This is pure gold, Lizzie dear!" A translation he had commissioned from the Reverend Sivert Erdahl did not satisfy him, and on June 21, 1929, he wrote to Saxton that he was making his own translation and hoped to have it ready by August 1.[19]

Even though the "folly" is removed from the title, it is retained in the motto on the flyleaf, a quotation from Luke 12:20: "But God said unto him, Thou fool, this night thy soul Shall be required of thee: then Whose shall those things be, Which thou hast provided?" The structure has been tightened by giving titles to the five sections into which the book is now divided. They suggest the traditional five-act scheme of drama, which Rölvaag was wont to present to his classes: exposition, rising action, climax, falling action, and dénouement. The Biblical titles suggest the apocalyptic nature of the parable.

The text itself has been so thoroughly revised that one can almost speak of a new book. Descriptive passages are expanded in the manner of *Giants*. The opening scene in *To Tullinger* only says: "It was a beautiful autumn day. The air was quiet, a clear sky above" (3).[20] In *Pure Gold* this has become: "It was already late afternoon; the day beautiful; the loveliest autumn weather imaginable; clear skies—the whole firmament only lazy, indolent blueness domed over a drowsing earth" (1). Passages that had been little more than stage directions have now become part of the story. The characters are more human, and even Lizzie is given a paragraph containing some insight into her psychology. The mixed American-Norwegian is in part replaced by giving Louis a rather more colorful speech with abundant expletives. When Lizzie demands ten dollars a month for her work as a hired hand, Louis's unspoken thought in the original is made explicit: "That's a hell of a lot of money" (*Pure Gold*, 49; cf. *To Tullinger*, 36).

One can understand Rölvaag's efforts to adapt the book to American taste, while regretting some of the lost terseness and authenticity. Critics capable of reading both versions have expressed varying opinions. Jorgenson and Solum, and his Norwegian translator, Charles Kent, regarded it as a great improvement, whereas his Norwegian biographer, Gudrun Gvåle, regretted the (to her) excessive "Americanization." Rölvaag himself expected a good deal from this book, writing to Saxton at Harper's: "The book has so much possibility to startle our literati that I don't want to submit an impossible translation. The color and the drama have been heightened, the points made more explicit, and the dialogue more interesting. It is also about one third longer than the original."[21]

In 1932 a new Norwegian version was made by Charles Kent, entitled *Rent Guld* and following *Pure Gold* closely. However, he also took the original Norwegian text into account "when this seemed natural."[22]

Most American reviewers were apparently not informed of the fact that *Pure Gold* was an earlier work; only the *Saturday Review* suspected that he had "revived an earlier and 'prentice work" or else was "taking a little rest." The anonymous reviewer missed "the serenity, the humor, and the panoramic spaciousness" of *Giants*, and while finding this book "dexterously and vigorously done," asked whether it was worth the doing.[23] James Gray felt that "the significance of the story diminishes page by page. . . . it is over before it has begun."[24] Thomas P. Beyer found alloy in the gold: "Rölvaag has conceived nobly . . . but he has been in a hurry."[25]

R. E. Parker admitted that it was well done, "but one wishes he had set out to do something else." In the inevitable comparison with *Giants*, he found it "more restricted in conception, less noble in execution, and less universal in appeal."[26]

Others were more favorable. Percy Hutchison in the *New York Times* gave it a strong send-off: "A story firm in its grasp, deep in its analysis, vividly unfolded and carried to a climax that is as humanly ironic as it is dramatically bold."[27] Mary Ross in *Books* found it "tenser and tighter" than *Giants* and *Peder*, "powerful" and "fascinating," though far from "pleasant."[28] Reviewers in such widely scattered journals as the *Boston Evening Transcript*, the *Philadelphia Record*, and the *Milwaukee Journal* gave it high marks.[29] Addison Hibbard in his *Creative Reading* (Cambridge, Mass.) gave it an intensive analysis as an example of a "Novel of the Soil."[30] The most enthusiastic review of all was contained in a personal letter from his old translator, Lincoln Colcord: "*This* is a great piece of work and no mistake!" He called it "a great work of art, and an almost perfect translation."[31]

A later critic, Robert L. Stevens, has expressed his appreciation of the book as "a significant work" in the naturalistic tradition. It is a study of the "sterility of the prairie" that "deserves a wider audience than it has had."[32]

Chapter Six
The Boat of Longing: Hearts That Ache

In 1921, within the year after *To Tullinger*, readers were surprised to receive a new book from Rölvaag's pen, *Længselens Baat*. They were even more surprised by the difference in tone: after the harsh, tightly structured study of warped minds came an episodic, romantic novel. Here Rölvaag spanned a young immigrant's life in Norway and in Minneapolis. It would be his only fictional attempt to join the homeland with urban America. The hero bears the same given name as in *Nils og Astri*, his 'prentice effort, and the last name Vaag, the final element in his own name. The identification is obvious, but this is not another *Amerika-Breve*. It is a fairy tale about the soul of the immigrant, which ends in midstream, long before he has won his princess and his kingdom.

The reason for this is that it remained a literary torso, labeled "Book I" and ending with a list of the section titles of a projected Book II.[1] Rölvaag was deflected by his decision to write what became *Giants*. Norwegian-American reviewers of *Længselens Baat* were intrigued to know what was going to happen to our hero. But, as one of them admitted on rereading it in English as *Boat of Longing*, "no continuation is needed . . . the essence is there. . . . The tragedy of immigration is here presented in full clarity."[2]

The book is noteworthy, as one American reviewer remarked, for its combination of two widely dissimilar strains, "the mystical folktale and the realistic novel."[3] Its four sections are neatly balanced between the two, with the first and last taking place in Norway, which embodies the mystical, emotional part, the middle two in Minneapolis, where Rölvaag's special brand of realism prevails.

In an unusual (and normally fruitless) appeal to reviewers, Rölvaag hoped they would understand that his characters were not "types," with which he had become less and less happy, but "people," who

were his chief interest: "Human portraiture has no end; it is as
manifold and inexhaustible as life itself." In an echo of Ibsen's
remarks after completing *The Wild Duck*, he writes: "Through long
association with the persons in these depictions I have learned to
know and love them. It is, therefore, with a feeling of regret that
I now part with them and send them out into the world. Take them
in and be good to them. They need it."[4] On the flyleaf he wrote,
"It is a mistaken belief that the immigrant has no soul." And to
mark its innovation in form, he subtitled it "Film Pictures," a
designation lost in the translation.[5]

"Along the Shores of Home"[6]

In the letter from Rölvaag's brother Johan mentioned in Chapter
3 which Rölvaag must have felt as a kind of consecration, Johan
wrote, "When opportunity offers, you should write a book about
our own, marvelous Nordland. . . . You owe your wonderful
Helgeland such a memorial."[7] The first section here is a fulfillment
of this challenge, though it does not follow the outline proposed
by Johan.

Nordland, with its glory of summer and gloom of winter, is more
than a setting: it is a character in the tale. The sea in summer lies
"dreaming," the waves are "indolent," "billowing lazily," "mur-
muring" and "purling" around the headlands and the beaches. But
in winter the same sea could "rage" as if all "evil genies" had been
loosed like "armies from eternal night" in the "darkness that hung
like a pall over house and home."[8]

Among the fisher folk, there lived the legend of a mysterious
boat that would be seen against the setting sun and then vanish.[9]
Those who claimed to have seen it were the unhappy ones. We are
told two tragic tales: of a pastor's angelic child who died of a wasting
illness and saw the boat as she died, and of a woman who lost her
lover to another woman and demanded to be rowed out to the boat.

Jo by the Sea and his wife Anna live in a fishing village in
Helgeland with their son Nils Vaag. One day the sea washes up a
young woman, an exotic creature with raven-black hair. Over the
winter she learns enough Norwegian to tell them her name, Zalma,
as exotic as she herself. Nils awakens her love by playing his violin,
and she responds by singing the songs of her people. One day they
go off together for a night of fishing. Then they climb to the top

of a nearby mountain to see "the sun dance at midnight."[10] Father
Jo takes action and sees to it that she is restored to her relatives.
In his desperate grief, Nils rows out toward the mysterious boat in
the sunset. He is brought back to reality by coming upon a tempting
school of fish, and the fisherman overcomes the dreamer.

From then on Nils is never quite the same: Zalma has become
the symbol of his discontent. He takes mad chances in sailing, goes
to Lofoten against his parents' will, and finally decides to leave for
America. In Lofoten, he has made friends with one Per Syv ("Syv"
is his nickname as seventh child; his real name is Peder Hansen),
whose brother Otto has emigrated to Minneapolis. Nils has also
been reading books at the fishermen's library, some of the same
that we know from Rölvaag's youth. He is stirred by Björnson's
poem from *The Fisher Maiden* (1867): "He was never given leave to
go."[11] On a Sunday walking tour to the top of a Lofoten mountain,
"he was seized by a grand and powerful longing to go away: away
to greatness, away to the greatest and the most beautiful."[12] Sitting
on a boulder there, he hears tones "purer and stronger and more
beautiful than anything he had ever dreamt of hearing."

When his mother asks him why he will leave for America, he
replies, "Because life is not here." He is looking for "the greatest
. . . and I want to see the most beautiful . . . and live it also."
To his grief-stricken father, he says that "if I can't try this, I can
never become a whole being."[13] They accompany him part way to
the dock, saying good-bye amid rainy hills: "His mother's hand
was raised. . . . The dusk and the rain were so thick that he could
no longer see the hand—only an arm that pointed up into the
murk."[14] In this touching farewell, we can glimpse Rölvaag's answer
to the Statue of Liberty: the farewell of Norway, reminding the
departing emigrant of home, tradition, and religion in its pointing
up to the heavens.

"On Foreign Seas"[15]

Without transition, we meet Nils after three months in Minneapolis (the year is 1912), living in a boardinghouse in south
Minneapolis, informally known as "Babel." Many languages are
spoken here, for this is a typical immigrant section. As a symbol
it represents the America that Nils met, which was very different
from the dreams he had entertained. Nils and Per Hansen are both

employed in menial jobs, Nils's being to clean floors in the saloons on Cedar Avenue. For roommate he finds a dissipated Norwegian named Karl Herman Weismann, who spends most of his time either writing poetry or drinking whisky.[16]

Oddly enough, this sot gradually proves to be a spokesman for the author. The dialogue between him and Nils seems to reflect two aspects of Rölvaag himself: on the one hand, as Nils, the young innocent lover of beauty, with all his childlike goodness intact; on the other, as Weismann, the embittered, unappreciated apostle of culture in a materialistic world. The Poet's speaking style toward Nils is one of lofty condescension, mixed with affection, a blend of styles, from low abuse to an elevated compound of biblical and literary reminiscence. The poems he recites to the wide-eyed Nils are Rölvaag's own, based on romantic ballad and folktale themes.[17]

The focus of Weismann's often befuddled preaching to his protegé is the folktale of Espen the Ashlad and his quest for the princess who is imprisoned in the Castle of Soria Moria. He sets Nils to reading the story and then recites his own poem based on it (in the translation, no effort has been made to render it precisely; instead, Thomas Job has created an equivalent poem called "The Ballad of Soria Moria"). Nils is moved to tears and, identifying himself with the hero, abjectly cries, "I'm afraid I'll never win my way!" The Poet has clearly failed to find *his* Soria Moria, and he asks Nils, "Can you imagine a person who walks about among his fellow beings and is not seen by them? . . . Or can you picture to yourself a man standing in front of a well-filled church revealing to his audience the fairest fabric that his soul has woven? . . . And there is not one in the whole crowded church who sees his treasure!" Of the contented bourgeois who have no use for his poetic gifts, he says, "They have their fields and their merchandise, their wives and their concubines, their great kine and their small kine, their Fords and their movies!"[18]

This whole section consists of vignettes, a gallery of characters who pass in review before the newcomer. Contrary to his countryman Per, Nils goes through it all innocent and untouched: when a prostitute tries to seduce him, he simply fails to realize what is happening. There is no plot, only a rather macabre picture of life in the Norwegian-America that sprang up around Seven Corners in Minneapolis. The characters range from the uproarious to the pathetic.

Nils can find some of the beauty of soul he seeks only in the home of Kristine Dahl, an older woman from Nordland. She lives in a small cottage by the Mississippi, under the Washington Avenue bridge, in the so-called Bohemian Flats. After eighteen years in America, she still mourns a lover who was lost in the great Lofoten storm of 1893. His violin is hanging on her wall. Nils plays on it a melody he had composed about Nordland: "With the sun's rays he was swept into an endlessness that was ever so beautiful."[19] He names it for the first time, calling it "The Boat of Longing."[20]

"Off Course"[21]

Nils and Per spend the winter earning money as lumberjacks in the North Woods. On their return, Per is lured into some unknown enterprise by a smooth-talking American and simply disappears. Nils is upset, because he had promised Per's father to look after the young gadabout and let the family know about his fortunes in America. On Nils's return, he learns that Kristine has been run over at Seven Corners, a fitting symbol of the confusion of the New World. She has willed her violin to Nils, whom she sees as a reincarnation of her long-gone Johan.

In general, the characters he now meets are birds of passage, rootless migrants, for example, a woman he assists in the Great Northern Station. He keeps her children quiet by playing his violin and helps them all get on the train for Minot, North Dakota, far out on the western frontier. She has been washed ashore on this little island; Nils ponders on how many such beings there are in America. He broods over his own guilt in leaving home and in not writing since Per disappeared: he could not bear to hurt Per's father by telling the truth. Nils finally accepts a job on the railroad and goes off to search for Per. On each city's busiest corner, "he would stand searching and searching, like a lone gull perched watchful on some bold headland round which the ocean current runs swift."[22]

"Hearts That Bled"[23]

When the letters from America cease, the parents are left to uncertain conjectures. Per's father Ole naively holds that in America they are so busy making money that they don't have time to write. One day he proposes that one of them take a quick trip across to find the boys. Jo is selected to go over and learn what has happened.

At this point the author interposes a chapter of prose poetry to honor the sea: "The sea. The great sea, faithful source of all unrest. It rests in unrest; it rolls on in unrest."[24] We are reminded that Rölvaag attributed his own unrest and emigration to the sea. "No, naught is like its longing. Without beginning. Without end. Restless as its heart; wakeful as its spirit." Odes to the sea were composed by Byron, by Björnson (*Arnljot Gelline,* 1870), and by Kielland (*Garman og Worse,* 1880).[25] Although this one is reminiscent of the older odes, it is based on Rölvaag's own wide and deep experience of the sea, whose billows seemed to roll through his veins.

Jo's dreams of seeing Nils are frustrated, however, when he arrives at Ellis Island without a guarantee of support and is returned to Norway. He meets a woman who has been in Minneapolis; she is sure she must have seen Nils, described as "a blond young man of medium height, broad-shouldered with blue eyes, on whom you could see that he was a good person."[26] This description, which would fit at least half the population of Minneapolis, satisfies Jo. But when he reaches home, he rows out into the sunset toward Nils's Soria Moria palace and is never seen again.

Story and Symbol

The lack of a well-wrought plot line and the many "caprices" (as Ibsen called the digressions in his *Peer Gynt*) make this one of Rölvaag's richest but also most frustrating books. The flyleaf tells us that it is about the immigrant's soul. The Poet enunciates the moral of the Ashlad's quest for Soria Moria: "Simply stated, it means that he gained his own soul, his own Sèlf. That's the most which any human being can win!"[27] Implied in this statement is the biblical injunction: "What is a man profited, if he shall gain the whole world, and lose his own soul?"[28] It is hard to know just how to take theology coming from the lips of the derelict Poet. He modifies the concept of "soul" by adding "his own Self," which suggests the theme of *Peer Gynt.*[29] Rölvaag saw *Peer Gynt* as a Christian allegory of salvation, with Peer finding his own "self" at the end of the play on Solveig's bosom.[30]

Whatever the "self" that Nils is seeking, it is not the wealth that America represented to most immigrants. The Poet drily declares, "So far no Norwegian has come to America without looking for gold." But when the fellow with the scythe catches up with him and asks for his soul, "he hunts and digs in every nook and cranny; but he can't find what the Lean One is asking for. No, not a shred of soul."[31] Nils has brought his soul with him intact from Norway, but he finds little nourishment for it in Minneapolis. He sees his calling in music, but at least as far as Rölvaag completed the book, he finds no opportunity to carry it out. The Ashlad "saw his own potentialities . . . God's serious intent with him. And when it says that after unbelievable battles he really arrived at the castle and won the princess, this is the folk imagination's poetic way of expressing this ethical truth."[32] This interpretation of the Ashlad's aspirations is hardly the usual one, that the Ashlad was looking for wealth and power, which to most people represents happiness. But Rölvaag is specifically denying these values: happiness lies in finding your own self, the soul that God has entrusted to each person to discover and develop.

Rölvaag was fond of this idea, as we see from his development of the theme of the Ashlad in his book of 1922, *Omkring Fædrearven* (Concerning our heritage), and the equation in *Giants in the Earth* between Per Hansa and the Ashlad.[33] When Raychel Haugrud (1974) makes "happiness" the object of Rölvaag's characters in their questing for Soria Moria, we have to take happiness in the special sense Rölvaag gave it: finding your own God-given calling and pursuing it to the end.

Two other themes call for interpretation: Zalma and the Boat of Longing. Zalma comes from the sea and goes to the sea, after awakening the yearnings of love in Nils's heart. She owes something to a short story by Jonas Lie, "The Wave" (1892), in which a mysterious young woman springs out of a giant wave, embodying (in Lyngstad's words) "an ideal, quintessential femininity."[34] She stands for "eternal unrest," and the young man to whom she comes sets out to sea, where he hears her "wild voice about love without an anchor, nameless and harborless." Rölvaag knew the story well and included it in *Deklamationsboken* (264–66). Zalma is more exotic than erotic, but she awakens Nils's longing to leave home and seek distant adventure. When he is deprived of her, he desperately rows out until he sees the vessel that was seen only by unhappy people. No known model in folklore exists for this boat, and the suggestion that it was inspired by Jonas Lie's poem at the end of *Faste Forland* seems misplaced.[35] It would be more apt to say that over the whole section rests the spirit of Jonas Lie's *The Visionary*, with its musical hero and its passionate description of Nordland and the mysticism of the Nordlander.[36]

There is a special mystique about Nordland, which should not be overlooked in any study of Rölvaag. He was himself convinced of the influence of Nordland's nature on the temperament of its people. The vast contrast of summer and winter, of sea and mountain, has left its imprint on the inhabitants. This is literary tradition from Jonas Lie to Knut Hamsun, or even earlier, back to Petter Dass, Nordland's "house poet" from the seventeenth century. It was celebrated by Rölvaag in his novels from *Amerika-Breve* to the last *Den Signede Dag*, as well as in numerous articles and poems, many of them appearing in *Nord-Norge*, the organ of the American Nordlandslaget.[37]

As presented by Rölvaag, there is a good portion of nostalgia for his own youth in it; besides, it is in a romantic tradition which gives the writer full liberty to employ such traditional devices.

To fall from the high romance of the first section to the realism of urban Norwegian-America in Minneapolis is something of a shock. We may have given too grim an impression: Rölvaag included many amusing episodes as well. But Minneapolitans might feel it as a worm's-eye view. It is undeniable, however, that the Scandinavian immigrant area of Cedar Avenue and Seven Corners, which sprang up in the 1870s and 1880s, was a patchwork of saloons and missions, of peepshows and Salvation Army, but also of workingmen's homes and churches, with Augsburg College to top it off.[38] Rölvaag must have known it well from his student days at St. Olaf and later on as a faculty member, when Minneapolis was the nearest metropolis.

Through the book runs an emphasis on the relation of creative art and cultural inheritance: art will not thrive in a society of the rootless and the insecure. Every immigrant lives on a Cedar Avenue, midway between something and nothing. A bill of indictment is here drawn up against a country that creates for its immigrant workers a Babel of frustration, in which it is literally true that "the immigrant has no soul." Not only is he rejected and ignored by the Anglo-dominated society, but he is, as Kristoffer Paulson (1975) has pointed out, the "invisible man," a term invented by Ralph Ellison about the American Negro. The immigrant is part of a hidden America, "adrift on a sea of American indifference."[39]

Critical Reception

Reviewers were ecstatic over the first section, praising without exception the lyrical and dramatic picture he draws of Nordland and its people. Rölvaag's growth as an author was commended and his mastery in the depiction of character emphasized. One reviewer wrote, "This book is deep as the ocean, billowing and struggling among changing moods, just as does the great ocean."[40] He found it wholly original, without parallels even in the literature of Norway. Several reviewers recognized themselves and their experiences in the life of Nils both in Norway and in America. Gunnar Lund found the book "extraordinarily beautiful" but noted that the "idealization" is occasionally on the improbable side.[41] N. N. Rönning said there is something "gigantic" about Rölvaag, a growing greatness, combined with the tenderness of "children's hands and children's songs."[42]

But opinions were divided and generally negative toward the American section of the book. Ager expressed it most vigorously: just as we have learned to love the sea—"brilliant in sunrise and at sunset, in storm as in calm," we are suddenly plopped down in front of a grocery store on the corner of Cedar Avenue and Fourth Street in Minneapolis. Our hero is going in there to buy cheese. "Alas, if anybody should be sent 'back where he came from,' it is the author at this point."[43] Rönning wondered why the author had not shown his hero the way to the churches and the immigrant societies in his immediate neighborhood. He lost interest in Nils after he gets to Minneapolis.[44] Ager called the book "almost a masterpiece".[45] An anonymous reviewer wrote: "When Rölvaag frees himself from the idea that he is teaching Norwegian and is writing for pupils, when he develops completely the artist in him, as he here so beautifully promises to do, we will get from his hand *the* Norwegian-American novel and the common Norwegian emigrant's metamorphosis under the influence of two cultural worlds."[46] Wist was less critical of the American section, finding Rölvaag both "realistic and considerate." He believed that "more concentration and greater restraint would make him into a first-rank narrator." His chief objection was to the improbability of the last section: "The normally thoughtful, cautious 62-year-old Jo the Nordlander would hardly take off for America" as he does or even less accept an old woman's tale of a blond young man as evidence of his son's existence.[47]

Some critics were aware of the kinship with Lie, but Ager was the first to point out the influence of Hamsun, which he deplored. Ristad brought out one of the most important aspects of the book: it demonstrates that "we are not just individual emigrants; we are an emigrant people with its own character, qualities, experiences, longings, virtues, and vices. . . . A people must write its own literature and that is what we are now doing."[48]

In a letter to Saxton (March 31, 1930), Rölvaag tells him that Nora Solum has roughed out a translation, which "will need a lot of work." "It is lyric throughout and is just as beautiful as *Pure Gold* is ugly. It is the novel in which I definitely broke with the plot formula."[49]

American reviewers, who read the book after Rölvaag's death (in what proved to be an excellent translation), found much to praise in it. It is recognized to be less powerful than *Giants*, but is given a position next to it. Critics apparently did not feel the same sharp contrast between Nordland and Minneapolis as did the Norwegian-Americans. Percy Hutchison of the *New York Times* called it "a tale woven of wisps of fog and shreds of sunshine; it is all Norse, yet thoroughly American."[50] James T. Farrell spoke of the many "charming touches that were characteristic of Rölvaag," concluding that the novel "will undoubtedly further cement the fine reputation" of the author.[51] Contrary to the Norwegian-American critics, Gerald Sykes in the *Bookman* found that Rölvaag "makes a real contribution" in his New World adventures; but in the "manner of the old legends he is transparently the professor."[52] Herbert Gorman (in the *Post*) held the book worthy of a place on the same shelf as *Giants* and declared that Rölvaag's books "were as Norwegian as they were American and as American as they were Norwegian."[53]

This book has been the subject of more critical study than anything else he wrote outside of his prairie trilogy. Raychel Haugrud (1971, 1975) has given special attention to the "search for happiness" in the quest for Soria Moria. Owen W. Jordahl (1972) has studied the folklore and shown how the narratives Rölvaag heard as a child have shaped his ability as a narrator. Paulson (1980) has taken up the losses of immigration and Ruud (1980) the clash of Old World and New World values. These many-faceted studies reflect the continued vitality and fascination of Rölvaag's near-masterpiece.[54] The reviewer of *Catholic World* laid the book down "with a sigh of regret." He was reminded of *Maria Chapdelaine*, the well-known French-Canadian story: "Its factual sadness is transmuted into gold by its spiritual quality."[55]

Of all his books, this was Rölvaag's own favorite. He frequently said, "I have put more of myself into that book than into any other." He attributed its emotion to the loss of his two sons: "If I had not myself experienced the tortures which a father's heart can suffer at the extinction of the dreams he has built around his children, I could never have written this book."[56]

Chapter Seven
Man of Letters:
Correspondent and Critic

The Rölvaag who forged ahead of his rivals among Norwegian-Americans by writing *To Tullinger* and *Længselens Baat* was in many important ways a different man from the one who had written *Amerika-Breve* and *Paa Glemte Veie*. The inner-directed, even self-centered Paal Mörck had thrown off his dark magician's cape and revealed the outer-directed psychologist and social critic O. E. Rölvaag. What had previously been an almost dilettantish concern with the immigrant's problems in facing a hostile America now became a broad-gauge attack on the failure of the immigrant to retain his soul, his self, his identity in the melting-pot process. But the central problem is now less the relation of the individual to God than to other men and women. The church figures more as a negative than a positive force. None of the characters in these books is pious: not Louis and Lizzie certainly, but not even the pastors or the church people who surround them; not even Nils, whose thirst is not for salvation but for beauty and fulfillment, and who passes by the only church mentioned in his neighborhood.

I have previously noted that Rölvaag remained a church member to the end and that he retained his deep commitment to the faith. But from 1920 on, there is a change in perspective, a broadening of outlook. He was in touch with the social and intellectual trends of his time: the general disillusionment that followed World War I, which a century of optimists had declared impossible, and the literary trend away from idealism to forthright realism. But there was also his bitterness over the concern of churchmen and parishioners alike with material values; and as the catalyst of all this came the tragic loss of his youngest child, Paul Gunnar, in 1920.

These factors would not have enhanced his writing if these years had not also been filled with an incessant literary production of a minor strain. His novels were only the tip of the iceberg: anyone who would follow his development and account for the sudden leaps forward, first from the Mörck novels to 1920 and 1921 and then to *I De Dage* in 1923, has to consider his incessant writing outside the novel form.

In this chapter, we shall devote ourselves to brief but hopefully enlightening comments on his correspondence and literary criticism.

Letters as Links

In *Amerika-Breve*, Per Smevik's letters link his new existence to his old and are eagerly awaited by his kinsmen, as theirs are by him. In *Længselens Baat*, the cessation of correspondence symbolizes the breaking of the link and leads to the father's futile crossing to seek news of his son. Rölvaag's habit of letter writing must have been established early in life, perhaps already on his Lofoten expeditions, but certainly upon emigration. It was no coincidence that his first successful novel grew out of the letters he wrote home. Both letters and diary testify to a passion for communication on the part of this unusually literate immigrant.

Throughout life, he was what his biographers have called "an inveterate letter writer,"[1] to which should be added that he increasingly cultivated letter writing as an art form. Beyond conveying current information, his letters are spontaneous, often vivid outpourings of his personality, unmistakably individual while adapting themselves to the recipient. It is reported that he could dash off a half score or more on a morning before beginning his daily stint of teaching or writing.[2] It is estimated that in his more active years he wrote as many as a thousand in a year. Nearly all of these were handwritten, in an easy, flowing, and highly characteristic hand.

His biographers, Jorgenson and Solum, gathered as many as possible of the letters and quoted them freely in their book, where some glimpses of his dry humor and deep reflection can be sampled. Regrettably, no one has so far brought out a collection of his best letters.[3] The most personal are of course those to his immediate family, beginning with his fiancée from 1903 and going down to his last years, many hundreds of which have been preserved.[4]

One of his earliest confidantes was the Reverend O. C. Farseth, a fellow Nordlander with whom he corresponded from 1908 to the latter's death in 1913. To him he could write of his longing to be back on the hill above Rölvaag "and see the weather-beaten sails heading north on their course as far as the eye can reach."[5] He could tell of the misfortunes of his first manuscript and of his disappointment with the attitude of church leaders to his work. He could also express his delight at the success of *Amerika-Breve* and admit that "I myself have very low opinions of them—there are five that are not too bad, but the rest are mere chaff."[6] In 1913 he revealed that he had thought of resigning and selling his home to settle in the North Woods.[7]

Some of his letters were addressed to a larger public, for example, the fellow members of his Nordland Society, urging them to come to meetings (in 1909: "We'll be eating fine, fresh halibut, but don't tell anybody") or telling about his own trips back home, at once nostalgic and humorous.[8] There are long series of letters to literary and professional colleagues, from President Boe to a former student like Ruth Lima (MacMahon). The latter he actually consulted about the psychology of the younger generation while he was writing *Peder Victorious*.[9] The roster of his correspondents reads like a *Who's Who* of the Norwegian-American community.[10] As he became involved with the wider American world, the letters in English multiplied, not only to his immediate collaborators like Lincoln Colcord and Eugene Saxton (at Harper's), but also to new outside admirers like the Jewish lawyer and poet, Gabriel F. Newburger, whom he met in Florida.[11] Each of these correspondents had something to give and received in return a share of Rölvaag's interest, which could range from saucy teasing to comforting warmth.

Although Rölvaag's interrelationship with his many correspondents remains to be explored, I shall present quotations from his letters to three women admirers who are not mentioned in the official biography.[12] All three had extensive practice in writing on their own and were kindred spirits in their love of Norway. I shall call them by their first names: Kristine was an immigrant of 1899, Signe of 1913; Mimmi lived in Norway.[13]

To Kristine he wrote (1922) about his disappointment over the attitudes of his countrymen, including the church leaders: "It is glorious to be giving oneself inch by inch for the welfare of one's people, even if one gets no appreciation from those who should appreciate. . . . If they wish to fire me, let them do so: 'It is better that one dies than the whole people.' I could hardly have pictured the 'Poet' as I did if I had not felt that despondency was overwhelming me. My despondency derives from the feeling that I am losing my faith in the very folk soul among us. . . . But when things are at their worst, I read the Old Testament: the prophets. Even they did not get an answer! So what right have we to expect results?"[14] When St. Olaf agreed to publish his book *Omkring Fædrearven*, he wrote: "I am glad again and cheery of mind. If we now . . . could get people to buy this wretched book of mine, I'd go out and sing although I can't carry a tune. Think almost I'll do it anyway!"[15]

When Kristine expressed fears about the health of her son, he answered: "The ways of fate are inscrutable. . . . Our youngest child, Paul, passed away in his sixth year. One day he took his wagon out about ten o'clock in the morning, as he had done hundreds of times before. At four that afternoon I bore him home as a corpse. God spare me from ever again bearing so heavy a burden! He had drowned in one of the neighbors' cisterns. Do you wonder that I can write about a father's and a mother's heart? . . . When Paul died, I was about to break down. But then I rose up against fate. That summer I sat down and wrote *To Tullinger*. Why am I now baring this old personal wound? Just to let you know that nothing is the hardest to bear."[16]

Signe was a poet and schoolteacher in Norway, when she married a Norwegian-American and emigrated to Minnesota. In 1925 her husband was killed in an automobile accident. In her depression, she expressed to Rölvaag her sense of kinship with his character Beret in *Giants*. She wondered what could be "the meaning of life." He responded with an expression of his own philosophy: "No, I know no explanation of life,—except to be good to others. . . . You shall interest yourself in all that is going on in our age, and you shall be good to all life around you. I think that this is the summa summarum of all religion."[17] From his sickbed in 1926, he replied to her letter of sympathy: "You, dear soul, look too darkly on existence. I would like to scold you if I had the strength. . . . Here I lay two weeks ago and saw it as the highest happiness of life if I could die."[18]

Meanwhile he had acquired another admirer in Mimmi, who began corresponding with him in 1924 after the publication of *I De Dage*—.[19] She wrote enthusiastic reviews of his book and gave public lectures and readings on him and on the book.[20] She was then a pastor's widow, downhearted and lonely. In the many letters

Rölvaag wrote to her there are words of comfort, along with active literary discussion. She sent him clippings and new books, among them a Norwegian translation of a Swedish novel by Hildur Dixelius entitled *Prästdottern* (The pastor's daughter).[21] The main character is Sara Alelia, a pastor's daughter and wife, who feels a daughterly affection for a rough and blunt, but unfrocked minister named Norenius. From this time on, Rölvaag addressed his letters to Sara Alelia and signed them Norenius: "I have all his faults, and then some."[22] To Sara Alelia, Rölvaag expressed many of his new opinions: "It is not important what people say they believe, but what they do—or better yet: what they are. As a parson's wife you will find this sadly unorthodox."[23] "I'm sure that the art of the future more and more will aim at psychological depiction. It is easy to make intrigues, but extremely difficult to create human beings. And life is so delightfully interesting that there is not a single human being who would not do as the main figure in the most exciting novel if only the artist with the glint of genius in his eye is there to catch the figure."[24]

The high point of Rölvaag's correspondence with Mimmi is the following letter of March 8, 1927, written against a background of her attempted suicide:

Dear Sara Alelia:

Uff, how sad your last letter was! Now I'm going to tell Sara Alelia a great secret, and this secret is the quintessence of all religion: We were not born into life in order to *get*, to demand. We were given life so that we might *give*. And then give a little *more*. And then again a little more. That is the purpose of it all. That is the answer to every riddle.

Sara Alelia is unhappy because she is not getting what her heart yearns for. But Sara Alelia should not yearn to *receive*. If she only could—and she can perfectly well!—turn her yearning right around, then she would find satisfaction immediately and her sore heart would be brimming over with a marvelously rich joy. Sara Alelia is like the deer that runs to the water to drink. When he gets there, he lifts his head and drinks dry air; he fails to notice the water; and his thirst is unbearable. Sara Alelia is like a singer who has been granted the most melodious gift of song. Instead of going out among people and singing until they weep from joy, she goes into a narrow, black stone chamber where she sits moaning, and then she scolds the Lord because he does not care about her."[25]

The letter is too long to cite in full here. Rölvaag goes on to compare her to a brook that tries to run uphill, to a rose that hides its fragrance, a wave that stops to listen to its own song, a star that puts out its light to save it, a grain of wheat that stops growing to save its strength, and with an allusion to Beret, to "yon heart that did not dare to let in the sunlight." "But what is the use of such parables? None whatever. For Sara Alelia insists that to be happy she must *get*. She must get the love and sympathy of people, and happiness." Varying his message again and again, he concludes:

"Now Norenius has preached for Sara Alelia, and now he hasn't the strength for any more. For Norenius is poorly and has no strength either for preaching or anything else. But he felt it was exceedingly *bad* of Sara to blame the Lord because the water was not deep enough where she walked through the ice. What if it had been deep enough, would little Sara then have been any happier? . . .

A sermon by Norenius."[26]

Rölvaag met "Sara Alelia" only once, on his visit to Norway for the Ibsen centennial in 1928. She survived him by thirty-four years, but she never forgot what he had done for her.[27]

Of Life and Letters

One of Rölvaag's favorite theses in his later years is expressed in one of the letters quoted above: that life is the central concern of the artist, that people are interesting, and that psychology is more important than plot.[28]

Beginning in 1916, he published a number of reviews that reflect his growth as a critic of literature. By this time, he had long training going back to his college days, when he ventured to pass judgment on heavy, philosophical tomes by Henrik Ibsen and Arne Garborg.[29] His efforts now were more modest in scope, and they nearly always included an appeal to readers to buy the books reviewed. Most of them were Norwegian-American: "I poke around here, looking at every new literary work as a historic event. . . . The climate is harsh out here on the prairies: there are not many beautiful flowers. When we happen to find some, we should shelter them in every possible way to show that we are fond of them. The only way to clear the path for a Norwegian-American literature is to find someone who will read it!"[30]

In a 1917 discussion of the prospects for such a literature he demands that means be found to sustain authors: "Only a genius, a true superman could create real art by stealing a few minutes now and then from his other work." He sees the task of the immigrant writer as that of

drawing images from our own lives, images that we can see and understand. . . . The fair palace of poetry has many towers, wings, and facades;
the wing we must see about raising is the one that faces squarely on our
everyday life. When seen from that position, the view will grip us and
our own emotion will be so strong that it can move others. For so it is
with the poetry of a people; it reflects life and transcends it at the same
time.[31]

Three years later, in reviewing a book of short stories by his colleague, Simon Johnson, he strongly asserts the position that Norwegian-American literature is in fact American literature—in the Norwegian language. After listing some major works, he asks rhetorically: "See if you can find anything *Norwegian* about them. I read them and find nothing but the language form. This literature deals with American life as we have lived it on the prairie and the forest claim, in the small towns and the prairie homes. . . . It is such a painfully stupid thing that the language should determine what belongs to a country." On his bookshelf, he has found some fifty to sixty volumes of such "American" literature, and he is sure the shelf will grow, proving that "there are still people who dream and see visions and are visited by the spirits."[32]

In reviewing the writings of his colleagues, he is always on the lookout for artistic quality and true psychology. He deprecates heroes and villains, preaching ideas instead of representing them, melo-drama of any kind. One writer who does not fare well at his hands is a Palma (Pedersen), whose novels *Ragna* (1924) and *Genier* (Ge-niuses, 1925) he took the trouble to slash into little bits. He begins in a fatherly way: "I don't know the author, but on reading this book one gets the impression that she is a good-hearted person. The trouble is she is altogether too good; and that is much too bad; for it keeps me from saying all the bad things I would like to say. If only it had been Ager or Simon Johnson—then I could really have let myself go!" After summarizing the outrageously melodramatic story, he declares that although the main figure is an artist, this book has "nothing to do with art, any more than the wax dummy in the store window has to do with the live person who looks in on it from the sidewalk." She could have written a fairy tale or a satire or anything else. But here she has "lied about life," which one can't do "without being punished." Because it is untrue, such writing is "immoral" and cannot enrich any literature.[33] On her second novel, he reiterates: "The author lets her sentimentality run wild and in that way she lies about life. Scarcely any sin avenges itself more readily; it is just about the only sin that life does not forgive."[34]

When Kristine wrote that she felt he had been too hard on Palma, he answered that he was fed up "with the lax conscience of our reviewers. We have had enough reviews, but no criticism. . . . I think my reviews . . . will make it harder in the future for anyone to review books without a trace of responsibility."[35]

He followed his own advice by giving thorough and often critical reviews of the more outstanding writers, like the above-mentioned Ager and Johnson. Ager's two major novels—*Gamlelandets Sönner* (Sons of the old country), 1926, and *Hundeöine* (Dog's eyes), 1930— win both praise and criticism.[36] In the first he finds figures drawn from life, treated with loving care and now and then with a touch of irony. He regrets the lack of penetration in the character study, but otherwise, "this book is Ager himself in his best moments, sparkling with humor, brilliant in its dialogue." The second he identifies as highly autobiographical, a novel of resignation. But Ager pastes a happy ending on the story, which Rölvaag calls "as false to life as anything can be." He excuses its shortcomings with Ager's difficult circumstances: "If he had had the time to devote himself to the material, he would have heard this himself; he is too great an artist not to perceive the false notes when he really sharpens his ear and listens in silence."[37]

Johnson was not as ready to accept Rölvaag's bantering strictures as Ager, being a far more sensitive and comparatively humorless man. The two had in common an aversion to the melting-pot philosophy and looked with distaste on the commercialism of America. When Rölvaag praised Johnson's *Fire Fortællinger* (Four stories, 1918), it was to him "a feast, for a man who had never known feast."[38] But when Rölvaag turned his appraising eye on Johnson's *Frihetens Hjem* (Home of freedom, 1925), Johnson was not amused. He resented Rölvaag's lighthearted tone, the more so since Rölvaag had by this time won fame. Rölvaag replied that while Johnson had become "more and more the romanticist," *he* had become more the realist. As Hustvedt (1976) has put it in analyzing this interchange, both men "sought to bring to the monotony and bleakness of the everyday some beauty and poetry." It is only sad that the success of one should have left the other behind, tasting the dregs of the immigrant artist's tragedy.

Once his own position, first in Norwegian and then in American literature, was established, he undertook to lift his critical pen to consider first the new major writers of Norway and then those of America.

After the success of *I De Dage*—(1924), he wrote a critique of Johan Bojer (1872–1959), his nearest rival in Norwegian literature: a cotter's boy who had written the most successful novel about Rölvaag's own Lofoten fisherfolk, *Den Siste Viking* (1931; Eng. trans. *The Last of the Vikings*, 1923). Rölvaag's criticism accuses Bojer of having been "in a hurry" when he wrote his popular novel *Den Store Hunger* (1916; Eng. trans. *The Great Hunger*, 1918). At the end of this novel, Bojer subjects his hero to a sudden conversion of the spirit (not unlike the one used by Rölvaag in *Paa Glemte Veie*!). The conversion is told in a letter written to a friend. Rölvaag declares: "Would that Flaubert or Dostojevsky had written this portion of the novel! It would take at least a hundred pages more to explain this man's psychology." He concludes that the linotyper was calling for more copy, "saying indecent words to himself and even over the telephone" since the publisher had to have it out for the Christmas trade.[39]

In contrast, Rölvaag treats the work of Sigrid Undset with un-adulterated respect: the first part of *The Master of Hestviken* he calls a novel of "the pain of life." He admires "the unconditional honesty" of her work, regretting only her prolixity: "Art should reflect life, as the fjord the mountain, as the sea the clouds. Art must not photograph." In view of his own sensitive use of the sex motif in *Peder Victorious* (1928), it is interesting to see that he commends her forthright sexuality, which he calls both "beautiful" and "tragic."[40] When she won the Nobel Prize, he was vigorous in approval.[41]

Knut Hamsun was the other major Norwegian writer with whom Rölvaag had to cope. A reviewer had even tagged him as "Hamsun's rival" in 1927. This was true only to the extent that they were both from Nordland and dealt with pioneering and the conquest of the soil. The reviewer noted in *Giants* "at times that light, tender, caressing way of considering his characters that Hamsun often gives us, notably in *Benoni*."[42] Rölvaag admitted that one of his problems in writing *Giants* was precisely to avoid sounding like Hamsun. The Hamsun style was easy to imitate, but dangerous in all its tantalizing glitter. In reviewing the novel *August*, Rölvaag noted that the hero "is a personification of industrialism: he is America come to Europe." He perceptively suggested that these late novels might outlive *The Growth of the Soil*.[43]

When Sinclair Lewis won the Nobel Prize in literature in 1931, Rölvaag strongly defended the choice and called the American opposition to it an "expression of childishness."[44] Lewis's books were mileposts: "After 1920 American literature can fortunately never be the same." In the age of "gilded literature," American books were for the most part a "timid, unnatural phenomenon, smart, but endlessly superficial." "Only action counted, and there could be no psychological analysis, for readers were not interested." Lewis's satire hurt because it was true, "even if he had to exaggerate it for effect."[45]

After the success of *Giants*, Rölvaag was called on to express his opinion on virtually any literary issue. He summed up many of his views on literature in a talk called "Books and Folks."[46] He there calls literature one of the mightiest forces that shape human society: "It acts upon life; life in turn reacts to it." The reason is that "literature is life, life condensed, life intensified, life often gruesomely distorted, but nevertheless life." He deplored the tendency of male college students to study subjects that merely amassed facts toward their future professions. "It is indeed both interesting and useful to know that there are forty or more racial groups living in the city of New York, but it would be tenfold more important to find out what dwells in the hearts of these groups. That no one can tell us but the poet."

He cites a long list of classic books that "humanity on its march down through the ages has warmed itself by as before great campfires," from Homer's to Mark Twain's. Although he considers *Main Street* as important for America as *Madame Bovary* for France, it is "only a negative" and therefore "the picture is partly untrue." But he draws back before Dreiser's *An American Tragedy*, in which he finds "not one decent man or woman." He said, "Human beings aren't just muck."

The most coherent and eloquent statement of Rölvaag's literary faith is to be found in his book *Omkring Fædrearven* (1922).[47] It begins in a polemic vein as a reply to an attack on Norwegian-American literature by an anonymous "S." whom Rölvaag identifies as a minister. He defends his own writings against S's attack and gives interesting summaries of the purpose of his four first novels.[48] Any one of them, he suggests, could have been the theme of a sermon. He then defines his concept of literature and its value. The first emphasis is on its relation to life: "All literature of any value must be a reflection of life."[49] At the same time it explains life, because the author must be one who can "see life" (in Ibsen's definition) and understand it. "In our day the delineation of character has become the test of all real art." But the artist must also have the gift of words, the ability to express the "inexpressible." He goes on to cite from a panorama of all world literature to prove that "literature is the mirror of mankind."[50] It is regrettable that the entire essay is not available in translation.[51] Only by reading the whole, can one appreciate the passion and humor of Rölvaag's literary temper.

Summing up: Rölvaag's psychological realism was tempered by an underlying goal-directed poetic idealism. Now he was ready to put his theories to their test.

Chapter Eight

Giants in the Earth: The Land-Taking

It is one of the theses of this study that the success as well as the inner significance of *Giants in the Earth* can be grasped only against Rölvaag's background and his most firmly held convictions. One cannot, as some have done, separate his work as a writer from his work for his ethnic heritage. There is less overt propaganda in this book than in most of his others, but the situation, the characters, and the plot not only illustrate his basic idea but embody it in innumerable allusions. His faith in creative aspiration is present in his characters, and the work itself is a creative presentation of his and their potentialities.

Rölvaag's characters are Norwegian immigrants, but they are also men and women, whose efforts to carve out new lives for themselves in the wilderness may be seen as universal. In summarizing the story and giving some glimpses of the significance that surely underlies its appeal to so many readers and critics, we shall also suggest some facets of Rölvaag's skill both as a verbal artist and as a student of human psychology. His skill had grown with each novel he produced, and after *Længselens Baat* he was ready to seize the moment when it came.

That moment arrived in the spring of 1923, when he read in the papers that Norwegian novelist Johan Bojer, who then had a world-wide audience for his best-selling stories, was about to visit America and collect materials for a novel about Norwegian immigration. Bojer had picked his time shrewdly, for in 1925 Norwegians were planning to celebrate with pomp and circumstance the centennial of their first immigration. He and Rölvaag had much in common, having both grown up among fishermen on the Norwegian coast; Bojer had, as mentioned above, written the epic of the Lofoten fisheries in his masterpiece, *Den Siste Viking*, just two years earlier.

Rölvaag was dismayed at the thought that this "outsider" would come and skim the cream off a topic that he had been preparing for in a lifetime of living and writing. He laid aside the projected continuation of *Længselens Baat* and asked the college for a year's sabbatical, the first and only one he would ever get. Once he had it, he secluded himself in his cabin in the North Woods of Minnesota and started writing.

He knew that this time he had to meet formidable competition, not only in Bojer, but in the standards set by a clutch of great Norwegian writers, whose fame was being spread in translations in many languages, above all Knut Hamsun and Sigrid Undset. Beyond that lay the dream of similar translations that would make him and his people known in America and the rest of the world.

What we now know as *Giants in the Earth* first appeared in Norway as two volumes: *I De Dage—Fortælling om Norske Nykommere i Amerika* (In those days: A story about Norwegian immigrants in America, 1924) and *I De Dage—: Riket Grundlægges* (*Founding the Kingdom*, 1925). These became Book 1 and 2 of *Giants*. We shall here treat them as originally published, as two novels, and consider the first in this chapter. In *Giants*, the first bears the title *The Land-Taking*, translating the subhead *Landnám* in the original. It is structured into six sections.

Landnám

The time is June 1873, the place somewhere in southern Minnesota, and the characters are Per Hansa and his family. In their miserable caravan, they are moving west with all their earthly possessions from Fillmore County, Minnesota, to Dakota Territory. Two oxen are plodding along, pulling the heavily loaded covered wagon and the homemade *kubberulle*, with its wooden wheels, that "might have won a place in any museum." Beret, his wife, is driving the oxen and takes care of the youngest child between fits of silent weeping. The plain and its endlessness fills her with terror, for she has none of the taste for adventure that fills her husband's heart with dreams of a golden future. The truth of the matter is that they are lost: Per is no longer sure of the trail that was to lead them through the trackless wilderness to the settlement in Dakota Territory where the rest of his company has preceded them. After they strike camp, he leaves his wife's bed to search in the moonlight. He hunts until he finds his friends' campsite, with fresh coals and a piece of horse manure; and as he crosses the creek, he finds a leg of dried mutton belonging to his friend Hans Olsa. "That night Per Hansa was good to his wife."[1]

In this prelude to the actual drama of settlement, the keynote of the whole story is struck: Per Hansa, the pioneer with his eyes facing the future, is unable to fathom his wife Beret's fear of that future. Even the children perceive the tension: "Too bad that mother should be so scared!" thinks the boy Hans, known as Store-Hans ("Big Hans") to distinguish him from his godfather Hans Olsa. But his mother's fears, still inarticulate, are deeply rooted in her temperament, and even Per Hansa's success in finding his way, and later in founding a home in the wilderness, is not sufficient to dispel her sense that in breaking away from their home and family in Norway they have committed a grievous sin. Per, whose thoughts are all of the opportunity that is being offered them, is troubled and even conscience-stricken at having overridden her wishes; but he is sure she will eventually see it his way.

This little domestic prelude is played out against a backdrop of the most magnificent scenery, a billowing, virgin prairie that reflects infinity in all directions: a blaze of sunshine by day and a silvery moon by night. The play of light and color is vividly described, and the half-playful, half-serious prattle of the children forms a chorus against which the author has deftly sketched the psychological problem that will furnish the dramatic tension of the book. Two very real human beings, who are deeply in love, embody the whole problem, not only of emigrants, but of mankind itself, on its way from sunrise to sunset.

Meanwhile the others have been anxiously awaiting them and are greatly relieved when they finally appear. There is bantering, a *skål* of welcome, and serious talk about the future. In this little group, Per is predestined to become the leader, with his quick mind and undaunted courage. He is balanced on either side by his old fellow Lofoten fisher, Hans Olsa, big and steady and slow of thought, and by Syvert Tönset, commonly called Tönseten, who is the comic of the group, eager and talkative, good-hearted but flighty and self-important. Their wives, Sörine and Kjerstine, complement their husbands with needful common sense and good cheer; they are not afflicted by the sensitive fear that fills the heart of the lovely but dispirited Beret. Tönseten has already built himself a sod hut the summer before, and the others now have to get started on theirs. Little more than appendages to the company are the two American-born bachelors, mostly known just as "the Solum boys," Henry and Sam. These eight women and men are the kernel that will constitute. not only the first Norwegian settlement, but the world of the novel as well.

In this first act of the dramatic tale which Rölvaag has so carefully structured, Per Hansa performs the first of his many exploits. While Beret feels a magic ring tightly closing around her, Per builds their home. He builds it so large that it draws the ridicule of Tönseten, but Per is already the fairy-tale hero for whom everything succeeds. Here we first hear of "the kingdom" they are about to found, and as the sod hut grows, so do Per's dreams of the fairy-castle home he will someday build. But to her the prairie is a threat—boundless like the sea, except that it "had no heart that beat, no waves that sang, no soul that could be touched . . . or cared" (38). Human communities that Beret had known in the past had had boundaries within which civilized life went on; here there were none, "nothing to hide behind" (37). Readers may recall Magdalene from *Paa Glemte Veie*, here portrayed with greater depth and sympathy, just as Per Hansa, with his love and good humor, surpasses the rough and cantankerous Chris Larsen.

The rising action requires that the settlers meet problems. While the other men are off to buy provisions, Per encounters a band of Indians, but instead of being frightened, he wins their friendship by curing an infection that afflicts one of the braves. One day the cows suddenly disappear, and some are inclined to blame the Indians. Per rejects this idea and sets off in search of the cows. Learning from Sörine that they were in heat, he goes to find them at the nearest settlement and brings them back in triumph, along with chickens for Beret and a young ox for breeding. The episode closes with Sörine's musing remark, "When lust can be so strong in a dumb brute, what mustn't it be in a human being!" (109).

Again Beret takes no joy in Per's success. This event, she feels, should surely have convinced them that this was no place for civilized human beings; she hangs heavy clothing over the windows and uses the emigrant chest, symbol of her old home, to barricade the door.

"That summer Per Hansa was transported, was carried farther and even farther away on the wings of a wondrous fairy tale—a romance in which he was both prince and king, the sole possessor of countless treasures." A lyric passage details all the dreams of the fairy tale Per is enacting: "A divine restlessness ran in his blood; he strode forward with outstretched arms toward the wonders of the future. . . . He seemed to have the elfin, playful spirit of a boy; at times he was irresistible; he had to caress everything that he came near."[2]

But at the very moment when his vision is most euphoric, it meets its greatest threat. The climax of the first book comes when he discovers that on Tönseten's and Hans Olsa's land there are corner stakes pounded down with Irish names on them: Gill and O'Hara. These are the "trolls" that threaten his kingdom, and he summarily does what a fairy-tale hero has to do: cuts off their heads—he removes the stakes and burns them. Unhappily, Beret becomes aware that he is wrestling with a problem which he will not confide to her, and when she observes the stakes, she realizes that Per has committed what in Norway would have been the blackest of sins. When the Irishmen come, however, they are unable to produce their deeds and of course can't find the stakes; when they start threatening, Hans Olsa knocks their leader down and tosses him into the nearest wagon. The rest take to their heels. The Irish move to the other side of the creek, and Per Hansa establishes good relations by selling them potatoes. He has subdued the trolls, to everyone's elation except his wife's. She only says, "We'd better take care lest we all turn into beasts and savages out here!" (155).

Per again takes off to trade, this time in Worthington, Minnesota, where the railroad has arrived. He buys materials for a net to the laughter of the rest. While he is gone, Tönseten kills an animal he claims is a bear, and brings it to Beret as a gift. When it proves to be a badger and they have to throw it out, Beret is further confirmed in her conviction: they have taken to eating "troll food." She even starts to pack their belongings in the chest to return to Norway, when Per comes homes and brings her back to herself by his unfailing good cheer (and a shot of whisky to strengthen her!).

Although the scene ends happily, it is marred by some disagreements with the children. Beret is approaching her next childbirth and grows ever more difficult to deal with.

As winter falls, Per moves ahead, as full of plans as ever, while Beret grows more and more desolate. Hans Olsa, in his solemn way, warns Per not to become "vain in his own strength" (203). When Per makes a pair of wooden shoes for Beret, she merely tells him,

"You could have done this before" (215). Her thoughts go back to
the sins she had committed, first in letting Per get her with child,
and then in defying her parents' opposition to the marriage. "Per
Hansa was a shiftless fellow, they had told her; he drank; he fought;
he was wild and reckless; he got himself tangled up in all sorts of
brawls; no honorable woman could be happy with such a man"
(224). But their words were wasted: "Where Per Hansa was, there
dwelt high summer and there it bloomed for her." All this she had
done gladly, even when he tore her away from her kin and her
fatherland. "Was there ever a sin like hers?" (226).

Her thoughts gradually expand into a wider vision of immigration. Destiny, the destiny of many, has brought it about that this
folly has been let loose among men, driving them ever westward:
"Now she saw it clearly: here on the trackless plains, the thousand-
year-old hunger of the poor after human happiness had been un-
loosed!" (227). She never blames Per Hansa, only that he cannot
understand "that she could never be like him—no one in all the
world was like him" (229). Now she is only a hindrance, like chains
around his feet, and she prepares for her death, asking to be buried
in the big chest. Per Hansa is aghast as the labor pains come on
Christmas Eve, and he shudders at the shrieks that issue from the
hut as he tramps around it all night. But she survives and bears a
boy who is baptized by Hans Olsa; the name is Peder, to which
Per adds Seier, after Sörine, he says, but also with a wider symbolic
meaning. It is a rare personal name, used as a cognomen by certain
medieval Danish kings, to whom it meant "victorious." Most important: *seiershuve* ("victory cap") is the name for a caul, which
betokens luck for its bearer; this newcomer has it.

So the first book of *Giants* reaches its happy dénouement, on
Christmas Day, 1873, after a critical first six months of pioneering.
One phase has come to its end, and with the first-born American
child, a new drama is about to begin. Per Hansa has got a precious
Christmas gift: "It looks as if we were going to have a *real* Christmas,
after all!" he says with a laugh. But the kingdom is yet to be
founded, and its birth will prove to be even more difficult than that
of Peder Victorious.

The Epic Perspective

Even in this first book, it is clear that Rölvaag has succeeded in
giving his theme a wider perspective than any of his predecessors

in novels of the westward movement. By themselves, the events are simple and everyday, such as might have occurred to anyone. But the framework into which he has placed them deserves to be called epic.

Each event fits into a pattern of destiny, meaningful far beyond the lives of these simple, land-seeking Norwegians on the blizzard-struck Dakota prairie. The plain itself is a major factor in this perspective: it is not just "a grey waste . . . an empty silence . . . a boundless cold," it is also "endless." Rationally we know this is not true: the frontier would be closed by the 1890s. But its settlement will have consequences for the world and humanity that are indeed unending. If it is not in fact endless, it is still spiritually infinite. In the words of one critic, Rölvaag has shown his artistic skill by making out of this feature "an elaborate symphonic composition" that brings with it "an almost unbearable sense of doom."[3]

Even while he was working on the novel, Rölvaag knew that he was outstripping not only his own previous production but also many of his contemporaries in America and Norway. He could feel, as expressed in his correspondence, that he had caught up with the level of the Norwegian writers who were winning fame at home and abroad with their often multivolumed epics of the common man and woman in Norway. The simple farm-novel genre would no longer do. He had already created many of the ingredients he could use: Per Smevik's experience of the gains and losses in emigration, Chris Larsen's vain combat with the "trolls" of the prairie, his wife Magdalene's inability to cope with her longing for home, Nils Vaag's quest for self-realization in creativity, symbolized by the Ashlad's search for Soria Moria castle "east of the sun and west of the moon." All of these went into the heady draft that became *Giants in the Earth*.

Although living in far-off America, his reading and teaching had enabled him to catch up and keep in touch with the new epic wave. The generation to which Rölvaag technically belonged—the one that began writing around 1905, the year of Norwegian political autonomy—won its chief spurs in the decade that followed World War I. They were mostly from the humbler ranks of society, and they raised monuments to their own people by making heroes out of common humanity. The bellwether may be regarded as *The Growth of the Soil* (1917) by Knut Hamsun, Nobel Prize winner for this hymn to the pioneer. It was followed by *Juvikfolke* (1918–23) by

Olav Duun (1876–1939), translated as *The People of Juvik* (1930–35), which Rölvaag admired greatly. Sigrid Undset (1882–1949), daughter of a distinguished archeologist, also won herself a Nobel Prize and international fame by her trilogy *Kristin Lavransdatter* (1920–22), a pageant of medieval Norway (trans. 1923–27). Finally, Johan Bojer made a great impact by his novel of Lofoten fishermen, *Den Siste Viking* (1921; trans. as *Last of the Vikings*, 1923). There were others, before and after, but their status was less assured and they are not known to have been a significant part of Rölvaag's reading.[4]

Aside from their settings in the lives of common men and women, these writers had in common a sense of the sweep of history, rooted in the past and pointing toward the future. In their striving for epic breadth, they tried to encompass a whole society with a realism that was not ideological but psychological, making the struggle of men with nature and with themselves the central theme. Rölvaag joined this company by fixing his eye on the dramatic story of the American frontier and weaving into it the conflict that was peculiar to the non-English-speaking immigrant. As he himself put it, the westward movement and the immigrant's struggle were the plus and minus of empire building. He found his formula by marrying them, that is, by embodying them in a husband and a wife and then "letting them work out their destinies on the Dakota plains."[5] In this way he could meet the standard of the epic realists of his day, seeing a closely knit web of everyday life through a prism that gave it broad human significance. It became, like his Norwegian models, the story of a people, his own people. But because they helped to build America, they were also Americans, caught up in the destiny of the new world, archetypes of all Americans.

The Berdahl Background

The choice of setting was determined by his own experience in South Dakota, first as farmhand, then as student, most of all as husband. He could have chosen a favorite figure of his, the adventurer Cleng Peerson, "pathfinder of Norwegian immigration" in Illinois and Texas (as did Alfred Hauge in later years).[6] Or the most famous of early Midwestern settlements, say Muskego in Wisconsin, as Moberg would later choose Chisago Lake in Minnesota for his Swedes.[7] He could have picked the last frontier, in North Dakota, as did Johan Bojer.[8] In the end, however, he fixed upon a spot some twenty-six miles northwest of Sioux Falls, not far from the homestead selected by his father-in-law, Andrew Berdahl. Berdahl had come to South Dakota in June 1873 as a man of twenty-five. The year is the same as Per Hansa's and the site closer to present-day Colton, the Berdahl's nearer Garretson.

In the Berdahl home, Rölvaag could literally tap a living source of pioneer history and thereby extend his perspective a generation back beyond the years he had himself lived, studied, and taught in the state.[9] Andrew Berdahl, who became assistant county auditor of Minnehaha County, was born in Sogn, and we do indeed hear of a Sogning community east of Spring Creek in *Giants*. The trek that had brought the Berdahl family to South Dakota had come from Fillmore County, Minnesota, and followed virtually the same course as Per Hansa and his company.

Rölvaag acknowledged his sources in an article in the *Editor*, stating that "some of the incidents—many of them, in fact—have actually happened; they are taken from stories told me."[10] Once he had started his writing, he felt the need to deepen his knowledge and went out to see some of the old-timers. He dwelt, he says, on the long trek, the interminable journey (the Berdahls had used four weeks on the trip), "the impression of the virgin prairies upon the different temperaments . . . the locust plague; that terrible winter of 1880–1881." Rölvaag's intense concentration on the facts is reflected in the available letters Andrew wrote in reply to his questions and in a study by Kristoffer F. Paulson of oral reminiscences and written autobiographies of the Berdahl brothers.[11] Like Per Hansa, the Berdahls were often mired in the mud; they started an informal school among themselves; and even a reaction like that of Beret to the desolation of the new place is reported: one woman "actually broke down and cried," while another (Andrew's wife Karen) "was afraid to be alone" and was in fact "never really reconciled to pioneer life." An Indian trail ran across their land; grasshoppers came like a snowstorm; the snow winter of 1880–81 claimed more than one life. The story of the rainmaker in *Their Fathers' God* was also a Berdahl contribution, though it could be confirmed by printed sources.[12] Rölvaag spoke of his awe at hearing the stories of the pioneers. Those who, like the present writer, have also listened to the pioneers, can only express our admiration for the creative treatment he was able to give these often matter-of-fact accounts.

Whatever he got from his sources was supplemented by his own invention: there was no Nordland settlement (although Andrew speaks of a "Per Nordlænding"); the ever-present similes of the sea are his own; and the depth of psychology as well as the wide symbolic perspectives are drawn from his own experience of immigration and its history.

Rölvaag's basic conviction was that the book was "true," as he writes in a letter to his brothers in Norway, "that is, historically correct." "Fifty years from now this work . . . should have greater significance than it does now."[13]

Even with all the care Rölvaag took to make his novel what we would call "documentary," he did not escape censure from his more literal-minded readers. One LeRoy G. Davis wrote to *Minnesota History* rejecting the absence of bird life, the breaking by Per Hansa of an acre and a half in one day, the description of the grasshopper swarms, and the snow tunnels in the winter. His conclusion is that Rölvaag was taken in by the inevitable exaggerations of his informants.[14] These criticisms were all answered by other contributors, including the prominent Minnesota politician Einar Hoidale.[15]

Mythical Perspectives[16]

In any case, the broad appeal of *I De Dage*— was due less to the fidelity of its details than to its symbolic and metaphorical perspectives. Per Hansa and Beret are seen by the author and by his critics as typifying everyman and everywoman. They live in a world that is no more South Dakota than anywhere else in a United States settled from east to west, or in any country where people have penetrated into the wilderness to make their home. There are strong overtones of *Robinson Crusoe*. As Defoe set out to show how life could be sustained on a desert island, so Rölvaag wished to show how a society can be created in a wilderness. Every new step is an advance that calls for joy and celebration; every reverse is a tragic setback.

In *I De Dage*—, the wilderness to be mastered is the prairie. The prairie is at once the resource whose riches are to be exploited and the enemy that blocks the intruders' way to those resources. Rölvaag has used every myth at his command to personify and dramatize this struggle. Hebrew-Babylonian folklore concerning the conquest of the earth by Adam and Eve and their offspring before the Deluge has furnished the title, both in Norwegian and English: "There were giants in the earth in those days . . . ," as we read on the flyleaf, with reference to *Genesis* vi:4. Christian imagery sees the menace of the prairie as an emanation of Satan himself, as appears in such section headings as "On the Border of Utter Darkness" and "The Power of Evil in High Places." Finally there is Norse pagan and folkloristic symbolism in the prairie as a troll, "which drinks the blood of Christian Men and is Satisfied." The pioneers indeed needed to be giants to battle these cosmic forces, and in the end, they did defeat them, but only by making the ultimate sacrifice.

Interestingly, Rölvaag was preceded in his poetic personification of the prairie by a writer who has not previously been considered one of his sources, the farmer-historian Hjalmar Rued Holand. In a work that Rölvaag cannot have helped reading, Holand's history of the Norwegian settlements (1908), there is a whole chapter devoted to a poetic characterization of the prairie and its meaning to Norwegian settlers; I cite a few passages. [17]

Deep in the heart of America lies the prairie, huge, endless, and unfathomable. For anyone who has not lived or traveled on the prairie cannot fathom it;—it is unlike all other natural phenomena and in a strange way has a depressing and provoking effect on the mind, as if it brooded on some deep secret. . . . Nowhere on earth does one get such an impression of the power of the invisible, and nowhere such a sense of personal insignificance and worthlessness. Therefore one becomes taciturn and introverted, possessed by corrosive longings, pondering on the riddles of life and human infirmity and inclined to religious fanaticism. . . . Such is its effect on the impressionable, impulsive person. But on the strong, firm individual its monotonous vastness is as inciting as a day of promise, a ferment of untested possibilities. [18]

In some ways, this passage could stand as a scenario for *I De Dage*—with its contrast between the two temperaments and their differing responses to the challenge of the prairie.

Chapter Nine
Giants in the Earth: Founding the Kingdom

When the time came to pick a title for the English version of *I De Dage—*, the literal equivalent, "In Those Days—," was unsuitable because it had already been used. The solution, to take another phrase from the same biblical motto, proved to be highly effective on account of its distinctiveness. But it also introduced an ambiguity by virtue of its archaic biblical language from 1611, when the King James or Authorized Version was prepared. The term *giants* makes an English or American reader think of mythological characters, and this is supported by the preposition *in,* which suggests that they dwelt *in* the earth. Many readers have assumed that they were identical with the Norse trolls, which Rölvaag uses to represent the antagonistic forces.[1] The Norwegian Bible, from which Rölvaag worked when he wrote the original, is more explicit: "Kjæmper var paa jorden i de dage." *Kjæmper* includes human giants or heroes, and the preposition is *paa* ("on"), corresponding to the Vulgate's *supra terram* ("on the earth"). That *kjæmper* meant "heroes" or "men of great stature" is clear from his reference to pioneer times in an article of 1922: "At that time heroes *(kjæmper)* were walking about among us."[2]

Although Rölvaag's favorite hero in the Norwegian folk tales was not exactly a *kjæmpe,* he did perform heroic deeds. This was the *Askeladd,* often Anglicized as Ashlad, the male counterpart of Cinderella.[3] We have already seen how Rölvaag used him in *Længselens Baat* as a thematic motif for his hero, Nils Vaag. Although the Ashlad is the youngest of three sons, neglected and scorned, he is the only one of the brothers who suceeds in finding the Castle of Soria Moria and overcoming the obstacles that stand in the way of his winning the princess and the kingdom. Rölvaag interpreted the quest as a search for the happiness that comes from finding one's calling, the task that God has ordained for each person's life. This is equivalent to finding one's soul or, in Ibsen's terms, of realizing one's self.

In *Giants,* it is not someone else (like the Poet) who suggests the hero's role as identical with the Ashlad's. It is Per Hansa himself, who is imbued with the vision of his own life as a fairy tale and himself as its hero. The term *kingdom* is often on his tongue, and when he brings Beret the deed to their farm, he says, "Isn't it stranger than a fairy tale that a man can have such things here, just for the taking?" (42). He dreams of the "royal mansion" he is going to build for "herself and her little princes." (46)[4] This is what America can do *for* one: make a gadabout into a responsible, hard-working father and husband, one who is filled with new and apparently inexhaustible energy. Whatever he turns his hand to, he succeeds at.

But fairy tales are supposed to end happily, and so the reader is taken by surprise when the last adventure fails. This is the story of Book 2, titled *The Founding of the Kingdom.* It shows what America can do *to* one.

The Founding of the Kingdom

The note struck at the beginning of Book 2 is the growing resistance of the Great Plain to the encroachment of man: "Monsterlike the Plain lay there—sucked in her breath one week, and the next week blew it out again. Man she scorned; his works she would not brook. . . . She would know, when the time came, how to guard herself and her own against him!" But the snag she had not counted on was the birth of a boy named Victorious (249). He was the promise of the future, however fragile he might be now: "Only a bit of tender flesh wrapped in pink silk."

The newborn child gives the settlers the strength to bear their first winter, which passes with social gatherings, including those that grow out of the informal school organized under Henry Solum. But again a trip is needed for supplies, and this time a storm comes over them suddenly, with Per Hansa lost and almost destroyed. Per rides his sleigh as if it were a boat, and like the author in 1893, he only just makes it home. On another occasion they decide to adopt family names according to American custom, Holm for Hansa and Vaag for Olsa.[5] Only Beret feels that these names as well as

Peder's are sacrilegious steps away from their fathers. When Per leaves her to trade Indian furs, she is left lonelier than ever.

Spring comes and Per sorts the seed he has bought with a reverence almost like that of Louis and Lizzie handling gold. He sows earlier than anyone else and is struck by a spring blizzard, but the seed still germinates and grows.

While Beret grows more and more unhappy, Per thrives as summer passes and the crops prosper. His field of wheat is ripe before the others: Tönseten busily takes charge of the reaping and binding, which becomes a community affair—the first harvest. Tönseten declares that the land of Canaan had nothing on this country! Just then the first cloud of grasshoppers begins descending on the land. The reference to Canaan leads right up to the "plague of the locusts," which would strike down their grain year after year from 1874 to 1878.

While the others lament this punishment from the Lord, Per Hansa pooh-poohs their beliefs; to Tönseten he says: "Stop your silly gabble! Do you really suppose He needs to take the bread out of your mouth?" (343). Per gets his gun, shoots into the swarm, and actually succeeds in diverting them from his field. Tönseten regards Per Hansa's attitude as "blasphemous"; this "outburst of angry rationalism" nevertheless saves the remains of Per Hansa's field. It reminds us of Rölvaag's remark after the drowning of Paul Gunnar, as reported by his biographers: "I could not make myself believe that God had deliberately pushed my boy into the cistern."[6] Like most deeply religious people, he had seen God's finger in every human event; but now "I began to see that much of what takes place is due to chance and to lawbound nature." One result of this forward intellectual step was that he could portray the rationalistic Per and eventually his son Peder with sympathy, and not, like Chris Larsen, as hardened sinners.

But precisely through this visitation Beret is pushed over the brink of insanity. Per finds her crouching in the immigrant chest with the baby Peder and And-ongen: "Weep now, weep much and long because of your sin!" (349). That night the Great Prairie stretched herself voluptuously; giantlike and full of cunning, she laughed softly into the reddish moon. 'Now we will see what human might may avail against us! . . . Now we'll see!' "[7]

An itinerant pastor, unnamed, arrives at Tönseten's hut and asks for shelter. Their meeting brings out a humorous contrast between the pastor and Tönseten: his first act is to reprimand Tönseten for his swearing. He calls the people together for their first service, in Per and Beret's sod hut; at the baptismal service Beret tries to prevent the name Victorious from being given to Peder. In an intimate talk with the minister, Per for the first time is able to speak out about their problem: he recognizes "that there are some people . . . who never should emigrate, because, you see, they can't take pleasure in that which is to come—they simply can't see it!" (385). The minister's sermon deals with the coming of the Israelites into Canaan and applies it as a parable to their own immigration. He warns them of the fate of the ten tribes who had forsaken their gods and disappeared, and urges them to be like the two tribes" who remained steadfast to the truths implanted in them as children by their fathers" (374). We recognize by his sermon another of the spokesmen for the ethnic heritage in Rölvaag's novels. Steeped as he was in the lore of the Old Testament, Rölvaag again and again sought sustenance for his goals in the history of the Jews. He even made contact with Jews to discuss their insights, among them the aforementioned Gabriel Newburger.[8]

The minister also reaches out to Beret, whose state of mind has become so precarious that they fear for the safety of her children. He requests that in two weeks she permit him to hold communion in their hut, using the great chest as an altar, the chest that is a family heirloom from the 1600s and that throughout the book symbolizes the Norway she has lost. Deeply sensible of his own inadequacy, he makes "The Glory of the Lord" his theme, and he directs his appeal squarely at the mothers: "If you, pioneer mothers, have not seen the Glory of the Lord, then no preacher of the Gospel will ever be able to show it to you!" When he places his hand on Beret's head and releases her "from the bonds of Satan," peace falls on Beret's soul. She overhears Hans Olsa offering to adopt their child and Per gently but firmly refusing; he takes on himself the blame for her condition, comparing her to a frail boat that should only sail in home waters: "The urge within me drove me on and on, and never would I stop; for I reasoned like this, that where I found happiness others must find it as well" (417). Beret comes back to her senses, feeling like one who has been away a long time, and Per is so happy he can hardly believe it.

It has been said, and it may be true, that at this point the story should have ended. A resolution of the tension between Per and

Beret has been reached; both have repented and have been absolved of their sins. But the larger struggle between man and nature is still raging. The grasshoppers are gone by 1880, but the author enumerates the many kinds of travail that still remain. However, men and women also have their resources: "It was as if nothing affected people in those days. They threw themselves blindly into the Impossible, and accomplished the Unbelievable. If anyone succumbed in the struggle—and that happened often—another would come and take his place. Youth was in the race; the unknown, the untried, the unheard-of, was in the air; people caught it, were intoxicated by it, threw themselves away, and laughed at the cost. Of course it was possible—everything was possible out here. There was no such thing as the Impossible any more. The human race has not known such faith and such self-confidence since history began. . . . And so had been the Spirit since the day the first settlers landed on the eastern shores; it would rise and fall at intervals, would swell and surge on again with every new wave of settlers that rolled westward into the unbroken solitude" (425).[9]

It would be hard to find anywhere outside Whitman a more eloquent tribute to the pioneer spirit. But Rölvaag has yet to show us the obverse of the coin: how the great Plain exacts its sacrifice for the presumption of man. The winter of 1880–81 is infamous in the history of the West: it looked as if the snows and the floods that followed would stop man in his quest for Soria Moria. The first calamity that strikes is that Hans Olsa goes out to care for his animals and is unable to find his way back until morning. This is his death blow, and the neighbors take turns watching at his sickbed. Beret uses her stint to imprint on him the need of conversion and confession: "It is terrible to fall into the hands of the living God" (494). When Per Hansa comes, Hans begs him to go for the minister. The scene recalls Mabel wrestling with Satan for her father's soul: he, too, looks to God only as he faces eternity. Per Hansa knows that his mission is impossible, and he is angry at Beret for instigating it. Beret may have been cured of her mental disturbance, but she has reverted to the stern puritanism of her childhood home. Per has moved farther and farther away from her, not only spiritually, but even physically. Per rejects the idea that Hans needs a pastor: he is a good enough man to be saved anyway! But when Hans begs him, and his own wife taunts him, he angrily sets off with two pairs of new skis, without even saying good-bye to Beret. He never comes back, and next spring he is found in a haystack: "His face was ashen and drawn. His eyes were set toward the west." The Great Plain had tasted blood and should be satisfied.

Per and Beret

Rölvaag admitted that many of his fan letters expressed pain and disappointment over the conclusion: they virtually accused him of mayhem. There has been much discussion by critics also of the ending. Since it is closely tied up with Per's relation to Beret and to his friend Hans Olsa, for whom he vainly goes to seek a minister, we have to look more closely at his and her characters. However lightly the theme is sketched in, we have had a warning of the coming tragedy. Hans Olsa says that Per Hansa "never would take help from any man" (25). And when Per whitewashes his walls without telling Hans, his friend warns him: "You shouldn't be vain in your own strength, you know!" (203). When Per half promises to go for the minister, Hans Olsa says, "There never was a man like you" (451). Sörine says, "We all have a feeling that nothing is ever impossible for you" (457). Beret flings Brand's words at him, with their Kierkegaardian overtones: "The Lord would forgive us then for what we couldn't possibly do—if we had tried!" (454).[10] And she even impugns his manhood.

By what right Beret makes this demand is not clear. But as Maynard Fox and Raychel Haugrud have pointed out, Per's concern with his material success has left his wife behind, unhappy and misunderstood.[11] She says, "You know what our life has been: land and houses, and then more land, and cattle!" (453). We are reminded of Louis and Lizzie, and of Chris Larsen whose concerns were limited to the material. Per Hansa shares none of their vicious materialism, but he does have his hubris, his tragic fault: in the search for Soria Moria, he has forgotten that he already had his princess. He does not realize that he has to win her again every day. He thinks that she is cured when the pastor gives her the forgiveness of sins; he does not realize that she had at that time become a true convert, a born-again Christian, which may have given her peace, but has begun to disturb the peace of everyone else around her.[12] Even Tönseten avoids her, since she will allow him neither a cussword nor a little cup of cheer. Per has accepted this, but has not understood it; in the English version, the author even finds it necessary to add two pages of text in explanation of her conversion. [13] So Per goes to his sacrifice, not willingly like Ibsen's Brand, but in an angry, unforgiving mood, an act that one critic has suggested is in effect a suicide. [14] But it is more than that, it is also a punishment imposed by the gods on the tragic hero. Rölvaag has tied together the theme of the "impossible" at the beginning of this section with Per's death: in America nothing seemed impossible, but in fact many things were. We may agree with Joseph E. Baker's words that "the pioneer struggle with the untamed universe may serve as a symbol for the condition of man himself against inhuman Destiny." [15]

The Norwegian Reception

After so many rejections of previous novels, Rölvaag approached a leading Norwegian publisher, Aschehoug, with some diffidence. The first draft had been written at the cottage in Minnesota. When the polishing was almost finished, he took it to them, and to his great joy, it was immediately accepted. The publisher decided to issue Book 1 in 1924 and 2 in 1925.

Kristian Elster, writer, critic, and historian of literature, reviewed it for *Aftenposten,* the largest newspaper. [16] "*I De Dage—* . . . has an extraordinary epic force, a vigorous narrative tone, a sober strength in its language, a grand simplicity in its images. It is a book that fascinates not only by its subject matter, but also by the manner in which the matter is exploited artistically and by the character study which it has occasioned. . . . It is a rich and warm and tender story, borne by a vigorous feeling for life and a refreshing sense of humor." Elster is impressed by how recognizably Norwegian the characters still are. "Rölvaag makes them neither greater nor better than they are; they are so recognizably our own. . . . He tells about them with tenderness and humor and is not afraid to let a touch of the comical fall upon them."

When Book 2 appeared, C. J. Hambro, critic and statesman, wrote in *Morgenbladet:* [17]

This volume shows how Rölvaag sees his work as a comprehensive epic about the Norwegians in America. We can safely say that these books are among those that will endure. Here and there they could have been more artistically shaped; but by their weighty subject matter, their epic power, their intimate knowledge of the conditions described, and their sympathy with the emigrants, they constitute a triumph for our literature.

Reviews were generally in the same enthusiastic vein. But the most important analysis from Scandinavia in that period came from a Danish critic, Jörgen Bukdahl.[18] He emphasizes the innovative aspects: "It is the first time in literature that the spiritual tragedy of emigration is treated in full by an initiate, by an understanding person who is privy to these events, by an artist who at the same time is a splendid epic narrator." After an elaborate analysis of the whole work, he concludes:

> Rölvaag's work is new and surprising—not least in its courageous honesty. . . . Rölvaag's book is a tragedy, because people do not with impunity break out of a cultural context that has been built by the struggle and strife of generations. These people wanted to escape from all the problems that pained and blocked them at home. But the problems were awaiting them on the prairie, and no one saw that except Beret, because they were so filled by the adventure and the challenge.

It is no exaggeration to say that Rölvaag's book became a sensation to the Norwegian public. But now his next step had to be that of finding a means of access to an American public.

The English Version

So far Rölvaag's reputation was entirely confined to the Norwegian-American community. Recent Norwegian authors had been translated into English in great number, and he had reason to believe that his success over there entitled him to a chance with Knopf, who had published Hamsun and Sigrid Undset. But Knopf turned him down, and he had to resort to local literary friends to rough out versions of *I De Dage—*. While these might be accurate, they lacked luster. The providential solution came with an interview in the *Minneapolis Journal* for January 31, 1926, reporting on his newly won Norwegian fame.[19] The statement of his literary and philosophical views and his desire for an American readership sparked the interest of Lincoln Colcord (1885–1947), an American writer visiting his sister Joanna in Minneapolis.

Colcord knew no Norwegian, but he had the advantage of a New England background, a record of publication (four books of stories) and experience in editing.[20] The major link between the two men was their love of the sea: Colcord was descended from five generations of seafarers and was himself born at sea off Cape Horn on a China trade ship commanded by his father. A study of the collaboration between them in the production of the English version that came to be called *Giants in the Earth* would require a book in itself.[21] Colcord's first service was to interest Harper's in New York, where Eugene Saxton became editorial midwife to the book. He then took the various texts produced by the amateur translators and reworked them into literary English. Rölvaag was lyrical in praise of the result and asserted more than once that without knowing the original, Colcord had again and again succeeded in catching its mood and real meaning better than those who did. Once each section had been rewritten, the men would confer and argue out the final version.[22]

Both collaborators had fully intended to write an account of what they came to call their "double action" method of translation. The first edition appeared with no translator's name, leaving reviewers to think Rölvaag had done his own; the title page was quickly changed to read "English text by Lincoln Colcord and the Author." In a new foreword Rölvaag named those translators who had provided what he called "a literal translation." But his deepest gratitude was to Colcord, "who unified and literally rewrote the English text." "How intensely we struggled with words and sentences! It would happen frequently that several pages had to be rewritten. But he never tired. His has been a real *labor amoris*. Were it not for his constant encouragement and for his inimitable willingness to help, this novel would most likely never have seen the light of day in an English translation."[23]

While Rölvaag was generous in his praise, it should not be forgotten that he supervised the translation at every point. It might be true as he used to say, that English did not "sing" for him, but he was by this time totally fluent in English speech and had a long life behind him of reading and writing English. Some analysis of the relation between the original and the ultimate English version may be found in the biographies by Jorgenson and Solum (372–76) and by Gvåle (368–69). Actual content changes are few, but the translation is less succinct and the characters have become more boisterous. The translation is a re-creation, in which the author has played a large part under the tutelage of a skillful native writer of the English literary idiom, American style.

The American Reception

In 1927, when *Giants in the Earth* appeared on the American book market, its author was immediately recognized not merely as a new voice but as a man with a new message. The book was launched as a classic, with a glowing introduction by Lincoln Colcord, in which Rölvaag's life was presented in the best American tradition of rags to riches. The romance of the author's life cast an aura of glamor on the book, and its extraordinary bilingual birth piqued readers' curiosity. In Colcord's words: it is a novel "so palpably European in its art and atmosphere, so distinctly American in everything it deals with."[24]

Yet the book could easily stand on its own. Its beauty and power made Rölvaag a man to be reckoned with in the American literary world. He had taken one of the major themes of American literature and history, the westward movement, and turned its triumph into tragedy. At the height of American euphoria, he had raised the question that few American writers had dared to ask: at what cost has this greatness been won?

The popular success was assured already at publication by the choice of *Giants* as a selection of the Book-of-the-Month Club, giving him an immediate sale of 30,000 copies. Critical success was assured by the serious treatment given it in all leading reviews and in an immense number of newspapers around the country. Walter Vodges in the *Nation* wrote, "This seems to me much the fullest, finest, and most powerful novel that has been written about pioneer life in America."[25] D. L. Mann in the *Boston Transcript* said, "There is a memorable simplicity and vigor about his story which place it in a class with the few really fine novels."[26] R. M. Gay in the *Atlantic* called it "a moving narrative of pioneer hardship and heroism, told with such obvious veracity that it makes almost all other tales of the Western frontier seem cheap."[27] Allan Nevins in the *Saturday Review of Literature* called it "half an adventure story, a realistic description of the physical facts of the homesteader's life fifty miles from anywhere on the Dakota plains, and half a penetrating study of pioneer psychology; and it is hard to say which is better done."[28] C. R. Walker in the *Independent* found that it "will give the reader a story done in heroic proportions of man's struggle with the earth. It will also give, I believe, a true picture of a great chapter in American history."[29]

There were few really critical remarks in these early reviews, for example, Percy Hutchison of the *New York Times* praised it as a "saga," while questioning if it is really a "novel." At the same time he found that it demonstrates "that we have not grasped the intensity and long duration of [the immigrant's] struggle within."[30] He found

Rölvaag comparable with but inferior to Conrad and Hamsun. Vodges also made the comparison with Hamsun: "He has at times that light, tender, caressing way of considering his characters that Hamsun often gives us."[31]

Rölvaag dedicated the book "to those of my people who took part in the great settling, to them and their generations." The great "settling" here translates the word *landnám*, used in olden times for the settlement of Iceland in the ninth century. In an article for the *American Magazine*, Rölvaag called the Norwegian pioneers "the Vikings of the Middle West," drawing a comparison that the immigrants themselves were fond of making.[32] It goes back to the very first immigrants in the 1820s and has persisted to the present. Rölvaag makes very discreet use of the comparison by merely making *Landnám* the title of the first book, rendered as *The Land-Taking,* and by making the English subtitle of the whole book *A Saga of the Prairie.*

The analogy of the picturesque pillagers and conquerors of the Viking Age to the modern settlers is tempting but of course dubious. In any case, "his people" were nowhere near as unanimous in their praise as Norwegian or American critics, nor as happy about the character he had given them. Those who were still wholeheartedly Norwegian and had a taste for literature were pleased that one of their own had won literary recognition, first in Norway and then in America. Prestgard, editor of *Decorah-Posten* wrote: "We all rejoice, not just on his behalf, but also on our own. . . . we all have grown an inch or two thereby.[33] Hanna Astrup Larsen predicted that "no one will rejoice more at his success than his own people, Americans of his own race."[34]

The prediction proved true only in part. From the appearance of *I De Dage—* in 1924 to *Giants* in 1927, there were critics who found Rölvaag's books suspiciously worldly and unorthodox.[35] The puritans were unhappy over the profanity, the sexuality, and the drinking, none of which seems to have been noticed by competent critics either in Norway or America. In fact, most secular critics would probably have missed these features of everyday life had they not been present. There were even writers who hinted that such a man did not deserve a position on the St. Olaf faculty. All such veiled threats were quashed by President Lars Boe: like a Rock of Gibraltar he turned aside every criticism and thereby won a battle for intellectual freedom in the Norwegian-American community.[36]

That Rölvaag was grateful to Boe goes without saying, also that the Norwegian-American reaction did not cow him. In a letter to Boe he wrote: "No matter how furious I get at our people—and especially at the Church!—I can't break away. A person needs someone to get angry at now and then. If I should leave my own people, I have nothing more to do. My own group provides me with the motive power I need."[37]

By this time, Rölvaag's problem was no longer that of securing a readership within a group "whose language reached no farther than their breath," to cite the Norwegian poet Henrik Wergeland, but of how to bear the mantle of greatness that had been thrust upon him. His book was sold and read with enthusiasm not only in Norway and America but also in Great Britain, and in widening rings in the rest of the literate world: versions followed as if automatically in Swedish (1927), German (1928), Finnish (1928), Netherlandic (1929–30), Hungarian (1930), Italian (1941), Danish (1943), Spanish (Buenos Aires, 1944), French (1946), Czech (1946), and Portuguese (1955).[38] No one has gathered or set forth the materials for a study of this impact. A bouquet of epithets from the Swiss and German reviews is overwhelming:

"An astonishing work! . . . A magnificent, sincere, and manly book, sound to the core. . . . A book that stands as one of the most significant of the past decade. . . . A new Nobel Prize candidate. . . . It has the enduring value of a creation by a great poet . . . a book of heroes. . . . Rejoice with me that we have once more a poet among us!"[39]

Fame was sweet and Rölvaag was not one to disdain it. In daily life he was the same boyishly magisterial type, as ready with a jest as with a profundity. But he was met with a new respect, and also with a flood of fan letters and requests for lectures and interviews that added to a growing frailty. His imagination teemed with ideas for more writing, but the race with death was already on.

Chapter Ten

Peder Victorious and Their Fathers' God

In October 1927, after a diagnosis at the Mayo Clinic, Rölvaag wrote to Colcord: "I have five more novels to write. If *they* would give me time and sufficient strength to do them decently, I would not care so much what happened to me after that."[1] Subtracting the two novels we will consider in this chapter leaves three he did not live to write. One surely would have been a conclusion to the story of Peder; he might have gone back and finished *Længselens Baat*; and he had in mind a novel on the pioneer pastor.

Despite increasing health problems, he did manage to finish *Peder Seier* (1928; *Peder Victorious*, 1929) and *Den Signede Dag* (1931; literally "The blessed day"; translated as *Their Fathers' God*, 1931). As sequels to *Giants*, they are often included with it to make a "trilogy," although in Norwegian they appeared as a tetralogy.

Giants reached its tragic but esthetically satisfying ending with the death of Per Hansa. But the climactic emphasis given to the birth of Peder, Per's only American-born child, with his ambitious byname of "Victorious," inevitably called for a continuation. As the representative of a new generation, he is expected to fulfill the first generation's dream of building a new kingdom.

Both sequels are novels of conflict, but no longer of man against nature, with its glamor of myth and folktale. These characters are locked in conflict, social and psychological, within a rural immigrant community that is trying to define new norms and find its American identity. In *Peder* we see Peder's maturation in a conflict with his mother that gradually weakens his bond with the Norwegian past. In *Their Fathers' God*, the conflict is with his Irish wife Susie, whose resistance brings out the obstacles to their harmonious union that rise from his lingering Norwegian ethnicity. Neither conflict is so much resolved as severed like Gordian knots by the author's fiat.

We shall treat them together as phases in Peder's struggle for his identity or, as Rölvaag might have said, to find his own soul.

As with *Giants*, the English versions are to some extent originals. *Peder* in English is by "Nora O. Solum and the Author," *Their Fathers' God* by Trygve M. Ager, journalist and former student, in consultation with Rölvaag.[2] Both show changes and additions that reflect the author's fine hand. Ager notes that he was "given all the liberties a translator could ask," with instructions "to 'translate mood and let the story take care of itself.' "[3] But he would hardly have added a whole page to Peder's encounter with Father Williams, including physical threats and the ringing words: "Your God is not my God!"[4] Nor would Nora Solum have expanded the last terse sentence of *Peder* from "Peder could not remember when he had been so downcast" *(uglad)* to a whole page of "a mingled feeling of resentment and depression," ending in an exchange of smiles with his mother.[5]

Peder Victorious

Peder Victorious opens promisingly with a perceptive image from Peder's childhood. He felt as if he were living in three different rooms: "Moving freely among them, he scarcely realized when he left the one and went into the other."[6] These are his three worlds: his innermost self, a "treasure cave" which it was his to explore, all in English; the world of his family, dominated by his widowed mother and the memory of his father, all in Norwegian; and the world where he lived with God, a "mysterious and secret" world from which even his mother (who had introduced him to it) was now excluded; this, too, was in Norwegian. How can he bring these three rooms together into one house?

Peder's attempts to sort out the unfused strands of his personality make for a certain confusion. In growing up he meets a succession of characters within the community, each of whom is anecdotally and often amusingly presented, but with little relevance to the main plot. In section I, the reader learns of Peder's reactions at the age of eight to his father's death in the snowstorm (1881). We follow Peder into the fourth grade in public and parochial school. Then, midway in the novel, we return to pick up Beret's story over the same period. Only then does the reader get back to Peder at confirmation time, when Pastor Gabrielsen is urging him, as his brightest pupil, to read for the ministry.

Woven into the account are strands of Norwegian-American church history and of American political history relating to the admission of Dakota Territory to statehood (1889). This textbook material adds historical realism, but detracts from the dramatic tension. History takes the place of myth; the characters have come down from Valhalla to earth, from high drama to melodrama, like the play that the young people perform in the schoolhouse, entitled "Louva the Pauper." In all its banality, this play represents the faceless American culture into which the characters are being assimilated.

"The Song of Life's Dismay" is the heading of the first of the novel's four sections. It is the title of a tune sung by a hired man on Sörine's farm. Although his real name is Ole Tönaas,[7] he is known as Tambur-Ola, Ola the Drummer, because he has served as such in the Civil War. The tune, which he sings when depressed, is a blend of an American war song and a Norwegian folk tune. Like the Poet in *Længselens Baat*, he is a frustrated artist. He flutters female hearts, even Beret's, and eventually marries Sörine, Hans Olsa's widow. His importance in Peder's development lies in his unbelief, which confirms Peder's rejection of the God who did not hear his and his mother's prayers for the return of Per Hansa. Peder sees God as "treacherous, sly, cunning," and is supported in this view by books he finds in Tambur-Ola's library, such as the works of Thomas Paine and Robert Ingersoll.

According to the classical proverb, the mill of the Gods grinds slowly "but exceeding fine." The quotation here alludes to the process of Americanization as promoted by Miss Clarabelle Mahon, the very type of an ignorant and inexperienced schoolmam. Lightly caricatured, she sees her teaching of English to these Norwegians as a mission to the heathen. Her almost hysterical worship of the American myth is combined with a sex-starved inclination to fondle her charges. Long before the advent of "bilingual-bicultural" programs, Rölvaag here put his finger on the cultural uprooting that was a major goal of the American school. Peder's disinterest, or even contempt, for his Norwegian heritage is reinforced by a total absence of instruction about his own background. In his school reader, there is a picture of a Norwegian wrestling a bear: "In his entire schooling in the common school this was the only information he received concerning the country and the people he was descended from."[8]

Miss Mahon's dismay at her pupils' bad accent does not prevent her from nominating Peder to read the Gettysburg Address at a political meeting in the schoolhouse. His Irish friend Charley Doheny is the other performer, rattling off the Declaration of Independence. Beret, worrying about the Irish influence, removes him to another, more "Norwegian" school, though here, too, the language is English.

We now return to Beret's contrition at her behavior toward Per Hansa in the great storm. She confesses to the pastor, who then tries to open her eyes to her own intolerance: "If you are to prosper and all is to go well with you, you must learn to find the good in your fellow man."[9] She assumes the burden of carrying on Per Hansa's work and soon proves to be the best farmer in the settlement. Her first idea is to return to Norway with their children, but Sörine reminds her that their adjustment in Norway would be as hard as was their own in America. She still cannot reconcile herself to the demands that America makes on her children, taking not only their bodies, but also their minds. Here "a people was losing its own self without realizing it."[10] She makes every possible effort to preserve Norwegian as the home language, but in vain. Even pastor Gabrielsen opposes her.

In the Song of Solomon (6:13), there is a cryptic reference to the Song of the Shulamite, which Rölvaag uses to refer to the love songs of this famous book of the Old Testament. Unable to compose adequate love letters of his own, Peder copies out passages from this book intended for Susie, his Irish friend's sister. Beret finds them, but does not recognize them as biblical and burns them, shocked by their sensuous contents.

By this time, Peder has actively begun the search for a mate. After some unsuccessful encounters with the girls of his own group, he turns to Susie, who returns his advances more lightly and boldly. Their love is confirmed when they play the leads in a schoolhouse melodrama. Beret watches a rehearsal through the window and, shocked at their play-acting love, tries to burn down the schoolhouse! But then she has a vision of Per Hansa talking to her from his picture. He reminds her of their own wayward behavior in youth and advises her to let Peder have Susie. She takes Peder by surprise when she reveals her awareness and insists on their immediate marriage.

The themes are familiar Rölvaag ideas, here functioning as guide-
lines in the lives of his characters. The struggle to maintain the
heritage of faith and language has become the mainspring of Beret's
life, but she is defeated on both counts by her son Peder, who has
drifted away from his moorings and sealed it by falling in love with
Irish Catholic Susie Doheny. Contrary to her behavior in *Giants*,
Beret has learned to yield, however reluctantly, and she herself
promotes the marriage. Peder has won his bride, but the omens are
not favorable. He is without his father's charm, can be awkward
and gauche without a sense of humor, and often shows a streak of
sullen stubbornness.

Themes and Comments

There are many excellently conceived scenes in this book. We
might mention the tragic "churching" of Oline Tuftan; Beret's
speech at the church meeting; Peder's thoughts after his first contact
with Susie; Beret's vision of herself sitting on a rock back home in
Nordland and watching a bird hacking corpses in the sea; the thatch-
ing party with Tönseten's usual bottle; the Fourth of July celebration; and Beret's vision of Per Hansa. There is also a vigorous effort
to promote realism of speech in an intensified use of dialect and of
English loanwords in the dialogue. These nuances are of course lost
in the translation. The Norwegian publishers felt obliged to annotate
some of the Americanisms for Norwegian readers, mislabeling them
as "vulgarisms." Such words as *fila* ("the field"), *krua* ("the crew"),
or *miden* ("meeting") were part of the everyday, unconscious speech
of all rural Norwegian-Americans.[11]

Yet it is true, as Rölvaag himself wrote to Colcord while working
on the novel, that "it won't have the sweep, the vastness, and the
lift" of *Giants*, "because the theme is so entirely different."[12] In a
discussion of his purpose in writing *Peder*, contained in a letter to
Percy Boynton, he defined the difference. While *Giants* reflected
the plus and minus of empire-building, *Peder* "deals more with the
inner side of the problem."[13] "So little of the story of the non-
English-speaking immigrant has yet been told in fiction. . . . The
giving up of one language and the acquiring of a new requires a
spiritual readjustment which forever will be beyond the power of
the average man, because it requires a re-making of soul." After
elaborating on the loss to mother and child alike of the break in

communication, "which is oftentimes brutal," he pleads for an understanding of "the heartache of that mother as she sees the child slip away from her into another world. . . . There is intimate kinship between the soul and the soil in which it grows."[14]

Rölvaag certainly did not intend this to be a book applicable only to Norwegian-American immigrants and hence of minor interest to others. He wanted it to be "a *document humaine*, one that should be true for all racial groups, more or less, and endure the acid test of time."[15] If reviewers did not always see its more general message, this could be due to their potential impatience with the immigrant's resistance to the "melting pot," as personified in Beret. But it could also be due to the fact that Peder is a less dramatic and impressive character than his father. However hard he tried, Rölvaag's understanding of the American-born generation could not have the same intimacy and power of self-anatomy as did his identification with Beret.

Peder is a young man in revolt, not only against his mother's dominance, but also against her ethnicity, her language, and her church. To Rölvaag, these were indissolubly connected: reject one and you reject all. In real life this was rarely true; most Norwegian-American youth, at least in rural communities, continued to speak Norwegian at home and remained faithful to Lutheranism even when the language of the church became English. Most of them married within their group (or the closely related Swedes and Danes). They did in fact communicate intimately with their parents and even to a great extent with their grandparents; to this day, there is much lingering ethnicity, as reflected in visits to Norway, renewed contacts with distant relatives, a blossoming of genealogical studies, and even evening classes in Norwegian.

If we look back on Peder's three "rooms" from his childhood, we can say that his "English room" expanded to fill his entire life: his own self is expressed in his ambitions in school, in mating, in plans for his career. The other two are simply locked up and gather cobwebs. His best friend and his chosen love are Irish, not Norwegian. He feels ashamed of his mother's English and the ways of his people in general. The room with his God is equally disused, since he gets the feeling that if God exists, he seems to live in Norway, not in America. The pictures of church strife and religious intolerance are understandable in terms of Rölvaag's feeling about the ministry in this period of his life, but are something less than

fair-minded or adequate portrayals. They are calculated to account
for Peder's revolt and his inner development. In spite of the title,
this is not so much Peder's book as it is Beret's. For all her unrea-
sonableness, she is still Rölvaag's love.

Their Fathers' God

Peder is twenty-one when this last of Rölvaag's novels opens.
Susie and he have been married for six months, she is pregnant,
and they are living on Beret's farm. It would seem to be the dawn
of a "blessed day," as in the pentecostal hymn by Grundtvig[16] after
which the Norwegian original is named. But the English title *Their
Fathers' God* comes closer to identifying the central theme, although
the problems of this mixed marriage have less to do with God than
with temperaments and ways of life. Beret does what she can to
keep the marriage together, but her very presence on the farm
deprives the young couple of the freedom of movement that would
be necessary to adjust their personalities and cultures to one another.
Without realizing it, she makes Peder more Norwegian and Susie
more Irish than they might otherwise have been.

But the controversy is also fueled from the outside. The community is divided between Norwegians and Irishmen, who differ
not only in language and customs but also in religion and politics.
Peder is politically minded, but chooses (like most Norwegians of
his time) to support the Republican party, whereas the Catholics
(including Susie's family) lean to the Democratic party. When his
own in-laws help frustrate Peder's political ambitions, the reper-
cussions on his and Susie's relations are inevitable. While we are
made to realize time and again that they are deeply and sincerely
in love, even an ardent physical satisfaction is not enough to overcome the barriers posed by social, religious, and political
incompatibility.

Rölvaag has made a sincere effort to be evenhanded in his treatment of the two ethnic groups. His portrait of Father Williams is
so sympathetic that one can only applaud the priest's tolerance and
understanding, which far exceeds that of the Lutheran pastors we
meet or of Beret herself. Peder becomes ever more aggressively
rationalistic and sets his own "common sense" against Susie's "hocus-
pocus," but he is no less critical of his mother's Lutheran pietism.
In the community, we see the effect of ethnic stereotypes in political

as well as domestic arrangements. The Catholics accept their priest's leadership, while Peder tells Charley that as Americans they should pay no heed to kings and popes. When Peder helpfully starts washing a huge stack of dirty dishes at the Dohenys', Susie flares up at the implication more than once thrown at her that the Irish are poor housekeepers. She responds that at least they have *more fun.*

The novel is structured into five sections, suggesting a drama, in which the climax is Peder's meeting Nikoline, the Norwegian girl he should have married. Nothing comes of it in this novel, but Peder now turns more and more toward his Norwegian heritage. In the end, Susie walks out slamming the door behind her. There are clear traces of influence here from *A Doll's House*, but the motivations are different.

The theme of the first section is a severe drought and the offer of a rainmaker to break it by "scientific methods." The rainmaker demands a prepayment of seven hundred dollars, and Peder is outraged at what he regards as an obvious swindle. He leads the opposition, but is defeated by Father Williams's authority.

The "cloud like a man's hand" (1 Kings 18:44) is also the first on the horizon of Peder's marriage. Susie, in turn, is feeling cooped up in a home where mother and son talk a language she cannot understand.

Susie bears their first child, and immediately the question of naming and baptism arises, as the title of the section, "And They Shall Call His Name Emmanuel" (Isaiah 7:14), suggests. The boy is informally called Petie, but Peder will permit neither mother nor wife to bring him to baptism. Peder is particularly opposed to that part of the ritual that declares all humanity to be "conceived in sin and born in iniquity." Here the church "had picked out the greatest, the holiest, the most beautiful thing in life and painted it the blackest of all wickedness."[17]

Here, however, he is thwarted in both directions by the two women. Beret secretly gets Sörine to come over and baptize the boy Peder Emmanuel in good Lutheran fashion. Susie with equal stealth gets Father Williams to enter him in the Catholic Church as Patrick St. Olaf ("Padraic" in the Norwegian original). The "St. Olaf" gets in because Susie has heard Peder laughingly report that he was a Lutheran saint and that they had even named "a great college in Minnesota" after him. In fact, he intended to send him there to study in due course. Rölvaag clearly could not deny himself this little joke as an effective bit of public relations for the college he loved.

Meanwhile Susie has had to go home to tend her father after an accident and rooms at the priest's house in town to be near the doctor. Here she feels at home, "surrounded by an impenetrable wall of goodness. . . . Here she sat among her own people, snug and sheltered in the age-old faith of her fathers. She was theirs and they were hers."[18]

Susie stays a long time at her father's, and when Peder comes to see her, she makes a show of affection before her family that only embarrasses him. "Here were forces at work which threatened to destroy the very ties that had held Susie and him together."[19]

At this critical point, he meets Nikoline, the girl from Dönna, a niece of Sörine's, who has emigrated because she lost her father, brother, and sweetheart all at once in the great storm of January 25, 1893. It is of course no coincidence that this was the storm in which Rölvaag almost perished and perhaps made his decision to emigrate.[20] Her impressions of America are not unlike Per Smevik's: "America is an impoverished country because people have not learned the art of enjoying life."[21] She silences Peder by unearthing that he does not even know who Mark Twain is. "What in the world do you learn in your schools over here?"[22]

She is a young woman of radiant personality and a sense of high adventure. At her first meeting with Peder, she makes him climb with her to the top of their windmill so that "our sight can take wing."[23] The echo of Ibsen's Hilde in *The Master Builder* is clear when Peder says to her, "You should have come sooner." She replies, "Why didn't you come and get me?"[24] Like Hilde, this girl holds the key to his real self; she could have inspired him, in Ibsen's phrase, to "reach the heights." She urges Peder to go into politics, but he has to admit that he is having trouble "driving the horses of success and happiness in the same team."[25] At their final parting, she tells him that she knows where Paradise is, but that the way is blocked by an angel with a sword.[26] When he asks to hold her hand, she puts it off until the next time they meet, either here or in Norway.[27]

Their meetings are played in a minor key, but the implication is clear. Rölvaag is reported to have said about Peder that "he must find his way home."[28] We may safely speculate that Nikoline would have lighted that way for him, for example, if he should fetch her back from Nordland and proceed to win his place as governor of the new state of South Dakota.[29]

The section titled "On the Way to Golgotha" opens happily enough with a string of parties to celebrate Christmas, including a jolly one at Tönseten's with the usual mysterious bottle that materializes on the table. Unfortunately for the reader, one of the parties is marred (as a party) by the entry of a new Rölvaag spokesman, one Pastor Kaldahl (suggesting Kildahl, Rölvaag's first college president and admired hero). He is long-winded and even more tendentious than the pastor in *Amerika-Breve*. After a long account of their Norwegian background, he tells them that "you have been entrusted with a rich inheritance built up through the ages. . . . Is it not your irrevocable duty to see how much of it you can preserve and hand on to those coming after you? A people that has lost its traditions is doomed!"[30]

Peder rejects his arguments: "We're Americans here!"[31] To which Kaldahl replies with one of Rölvaag's many biological similes: "Does the leopard change his spots by coming into new pastures?" Peder believes in America as a new foundation where "the whole structure must be new."[32] But Kaldahl reminds him that many of its timbers are brought from far away, some even from Norway. That evening Gjermund Dahl, the old county commissioner, talks seriously to Peder about becoming a candidate for his position. Peder is fired by what he feels to be a call, a call to leadership. But Susie is disinterested, and after a bitter quarrel, they move even farther apart.

Coming home one evening, they find Beret in the yard, where she has slipped and broken her leg. Sensing that it is the end, she makes her will in a deeply felt scene. She provides that Peder may not sell the farm out of the family as long as any one of them wants it: "This farm has cost much more than money can ever pay. . . . I like to see it remain in Per Hansa's family."[33] In the pastor's presence, she confesses to having had Pete baptized secretly. Susie flings herself out of the room in a fury, without revealing her own underhandedness. For once Peder thinks seriously about his mother's concern for him: "Her foresight, her concern . . . had drawn the circle of reality in which, up till now, he had been moving."[34] He now recalls her warning when he married Susie: "We don't keep wheat and potatoes in the same bin."[35]

Susie falls ill after a miscarriage, and Peder tries to restore their relationship. He talks about their going together to the "end of the world" where their "blessed day" will last forever. Even so he cannot restrain himself from ridiculing the black marker given her at the Ash Wednesday service. When the 1896 campaign opens, Peder goes all out against William Jennings Bryan in his own campaign for county commissioner. At one of the meetings, his opponent spills the information of Petie's Catholic baptism. Peder goes home and tears down his wife's sacred symbols, grinding them under his heel. Next morning she is gone with their child, leaving a note in which she says: "Now I have been at the End of the World and seen how it looks there. I will never come again, for there everything is accursed. Lord help a person who gets that kind of Blessed Day! I recall a sacred word: Father forgive them, and I say it, not that it will do you any good."[36]

Comment and Reception

The opening episode about the rainmaker is historical even down to the name of the charlatan involved, Mr. Jewell. Minnehaha County in South Dakota hired him, rather more cautiously than in the book, with an advance of only two hundred dollars. No rain came, and so he lost the four hundred dollars that would have been his if half an inch had appeared within the given time.[37]

The rest of the book is a distillate of Rölvaag's experience with the second generation, especially his own students at St. Olaf College. To one of them, Ruth Lima (McMahon), who had worked on the translation of *Giants*, he even wrote asking for help on "second-generation psychology": "How largely did you feel Norwegian, and how much of you was American? And this: when were you the one, when the other?"[38] As for Nikoline, she was Rölvaag's dream girl, the spirit of Nordland. He had already pictured himself in Nils Vaag, and it is significant that Nikoline is the feminine counterpart of Nils (from Nikolaus). That Peder became a Republican is accounted for by the fact that Rölvaag voted that party (in 1896, a bit prematurely, even before he was legally a citizen).[39] In that election, most Norwegian farmers voted Populist, including the Berdahl family, who would furnish him with a wife some years later. (Karl Rölvaag, his son, who became Democratic-Farmer-Labor governor of Minnesota, has assured me that *his* liberal politics came from his mother's family.)[40]

Rölvaag was well aware that his book would be controversial, and he wrote to his wife from Florida that he feared it would be a "flop." "It goes hard on both Protestant and Catholic. With these two mighty forces opposed to you, you have the current against you—decidedly. 'But a fool must follow his natural bent.' I have never written books for money, and don't intend to do it."[41] He was also aware that the puritans among his own people who had begun looking on his books with a jaundiced eye might find his frank treatment of sexuality and his use of the Song of Songs blasphemous and immoral.

Much of the criticism that could indeed have been leveled at the book was silenced by Rölvaag's death simultaneously with its appearance. In a letter shortly after his death, President Boe denied that Peder was voicing Rölvaag's sentiments; if anyone did, it was Beret. But "in a larger way" Rölvaag was not giving expression to his opinions. "The characters he deals with had to have their say through him, whether he wanted it or not."[42]

Rölvaag's intuition proved to be right, but not necessarily because of its controversial aspects. While Norwegian and Norwegian-American reviewers wrote about it with some sympathy, American reviewers found it "superficial" (Alice Beal Parsons in *Books*),[43] not "convincing" *(Boston Transcript)*,[44] "disappointing" *(Nation)*,[45] "balderdash" *(Buffalo News)*.[46] The reviewer of the *New York Sun* (Fred T. Marsh) noted Rölvaag's sympathy with Peder and Beret, and commended its lack of propaganda, which "lends a certain measure of strength to a novel which has no other claim to distinction."[47] Only the *New York Times* appears to have understood its message: "If Rölvaag is right—and he convinces one that he is—then that fond dream of the 'melting pot' went into the discard during the very years when it was most vigorously being talked. . . . Those interested in American evolution will find much to ponder in this frank study."[48] It is clear that neither the reviewers nor the public were ready for such disillusioning studies as would come with Glazer and Moynihan's *Beyond the Melting Pot*.[49] While *Giants* sold 78,616 copies and *Peder*, 47,252, in their first year, *Their Fathers' God* reached only 14,629 that year and was then remaindered.[50]

One reviewer (Fadiman) referred to the characters in these books as "diminished giants."[51] This only makes them human, and the human problems of Peder and his generation, as seen by Rölvaag, are still relevant wherever there are immigrants and refugees. "In this book," writes Gudrun Gvåle with great insight, Rölvaag embedded more of his philosophy of culture than in any other of his novels. It has become "an artistic illustration of his book *About Our Ancestral Heritage*."[52]

Chapter Eleven

The Rölvaag Legacy: From Norway with Love

It has been our intention to present, within the format allowed, as much of the whole man Rölvaag as possible. His story is exemplary in so many ways: as the poor immigrant boy who made good; as the fisher who rose to fame by his pen; as the foreign writer who made an enduring niche for himself in American literature. We must cease looking at him as the one-novel writer and see his life work both steadily and whole. More than anyone else in America, he became the literary interpreter of the immigrant as a special kind of human being. Many who had used the word *immigrant* as synonymous with *foreigner,* both as pejorative terms, were through his writings encouraged to glimpse a new vision of the human beings behind these clichés. It would be banal to say that he showed that immigrants were human beings; what he really did was to outline in precise terms just what kind of human beings they were. He did this not as historian or sociologist or political scientist. Through his imagination and his practiced pen, he was able to synthesize all of these aspects into whole human beings. This he could do because he himself was no ordinary person, but a genius in whose retort romance could fuse with reality to create convincing and fascinating characters symbolizing the many million immigrants who helped build America. Such people as Per Hansa and Beret, Nils Vaag and Peder Victorious, are more real to his readers than most of their friends; indeed, they *are* friends.

In this final chapter, we shall discuss some aspects of his work that throw light on his contribution to the life and literature of his two countries.

Rölvaag as Historian

History was one of Rölvaag's passions, but primarily for the story in it. He often said that every man and woman had a story that

111

could be made interesting if the right person were found to tell it.[1] But no such story was to be told merely for entertainment, however needful this might be to keep the reader or listener interested. His view of history was, as Kenneth Bjork (1940) has put it, a "romantic-heroic" one, belonging to the early nineteenth century.[2] He did not master the special techniques of the professional historian, and yet he became the promoter and sponsor of the Norwegian-American Historical Association, whose work has repeatedly been recognized as wholly professional. His agitation was borne by the same filiopietistic enthusiasm that has created parallel organizations among many American ethnic or local groups. But he did recognize his limitations in this respect and helped to install in the editor's office a man who would bring all the weight of an experienced and knowledgeable historian to guarantee that the publications of the Association would *not* be filiopietistic, but objective. This was Theodore C. Blegen, who would become not only a leading historian of immigration from Norway, but also of the state of Minnesota.[3]

What the Norwegian-American Historical Association owes to the enthusiasm of Rölvaag has been well documented by Bjork,— Blegen's successor—in an article on "The Unknown Rölvaag" (1940).[4] Rölvaag's ethnic mission had engaged him in active work for various organizations to preserve the Norwegian language, but with the formation of the NAHA after the Norse-American Centennial in 1925, he threw himself into the work as secretary of an association to render the history of his people into English. Previously he had insisted that only by preserving Norwegian could they retain their leavening influence. But he now saw that only by telling the Norwegian-American story in English could new generations learn about the history of their forebears and find pride in it. Only so can we explain all the precious time he spent on private and public correspondence, in endless meetings, and in organizing and stocking the archive that became a part of the library at St. Olaf College that would one day be named after him.

Poems and Stories

In *Boat of Longing,* Nils Vaag is entranced by the poetry of his alcoholic roommate Weismann.[5] In his naiveté, he cannot restrain himself from asking, "How do you go about making poetry?" The poet scornfully replies, "Why don't you ask Earth how the flowers grow?"[6] From time to time, poems did grow in Rölvaag's mind, and some of the best may be the six he interwove with the narrative of *Boat of Longing*. Such interweaving harks back to Björnson's peasant novels, especially *Arne* (1861), and the style is also reminiscent.[7] Most of Rölvaag's poems are, like these, in a ballad style, mood poetry in the romantic tradition. In *Boat of Longing,* there is a rhymed version of the folktale of Soria Moria, embodying a major theme of the novel.[8] Poetry is for Nils, together with his music, an escape from his sordid surroundings.

Rölvaag began writing poetry at least in his college days and continued down to the last year of his life. He left behind some seventy-five poems, less than half of them published.[9] Some appeared in his readers, others in such journals as *Nord-Norge* and the Christmas annual *Jul i Vesterheimen.* Some were humorous or occasional, intended for the eyes of friends and family. Others embodied themes dear to Rölvaag's heart, above all, nature and God: poems on the prairie, the forest, the sea; on spring or autumn; on Christmas and Easter. Some were nostalgic, taking him back to home and mother in Nordland;[10] others were love poems.

One of these appears in *Boat of Longing* as "Nocturne," but the English text (by Thomas Job), however charming, does not fulfill Rölvaag's intention.[11] In a note on the manuscript, he wrote, "This is written to prove that it is possible to infuse into a few lines more unbridled eroticism than in many printed pages of the crassest content—in prose."[12] The poem is printed below, with my more exact, if less poetic rendition:

Før syndefaldet.

Netop her paa heiens brem
raster vi i denne kveld;
bjørnens hule blir vor seng,
klippens bløte mos vor feld.

La mig hvile paa din arm
med mit hode tæt til dit,
føle hjertet i din barm
slaa i kraftig takt med mit!

La mig skue øiets glans,
stryke ømt dit bløte kind,

gi mig hen foruten sans,
vildt som viddens vilde hind!

Nyn mig saa en melodi,
sagte kun—nei ikke syng!
Læg saa livets løfter i,
bløtt som vaarvind gjennem lyng!

Kom saa Nat og hyll os ind,
gjem os, glem os, væk os ei;
solens friske morgenvind
skal nok til os finde vei![13]

Before the Fall

Here upon the highland's brim
We will rest this very eve;
Let the bear's lair be our bed,
Tender moss will be our couch.

Let me rest upon your arm
With my head close up to yours,
Feel the heart within your breast
Strongly beat in time with mine!

Let me view your sparkling eyes,
Gently stroke your tender cheeks,
Give myself without reserve,
Wildly as the untamed hind!

Hum me then a melody,
Softly, softly—do not sing!
Fill it with life's promise fair,
Gently as the winds of spring!

Come then, Night, and wrap us round,
Hide us, bide us, wake us not;
Sunrise breezes briskly roused
Will surely find us on their path!

Rölvaag, we are reminded, rejected the "crass" realism of a Dreiser,
while accepting that of a Sinclair Lewis. In 1923 he selected a
number of his poems and made a fair copy of them, evidently
intending to publish an anthology. But nothing came of it.

Poetic prose was more to his taste than verse. His first attempt to render the impression made on him by the prairie was a piece called "Moods from the Prairie" (1913), describing each of the four seasons.[14] This appeared in the Christmas annual *Jul i Vesterheimen,* as did most of the short stories he wrote.[15] An exception was "White Bears and Grey Bears," labeled "an Indian fairytale." Obviously it was a Norwegian-American fable intended to show that "white bears" (Norwegians) did not turn gray just by moving into the land of the "grey bears."[16] Another mood piece was labeled "old legend," and bore the title "When the Snow Drifts Down at Christmastide."[17]

The remaining half dozen or so stories are in the nature of episodes from Norwegian-American life, comparable to some that he used in his novels. They are humorous in tone and deal with marital and congregational conflicts in a rural setting. One is autobiographical, "Bright Morning and Wet Evening," the story of three inseparable fishing companions in the Minnesota north woods and their adventures.[18] After Rölvaag's death, his stories were collected in a volume published by Augsburg Publishing House, the publisher also of *Jul i Vesterheimen.*[19] Two of these have been translated by Solveig Tweet (Zempel), but not yet published.[20] While the short stories are in the tradition of Hans Aanrud's tales of Norwegian folk life, their tone of tolerant satire of human foible is unmistakably Rölvaag's. As a short story writer, however, he did not equal Ager at his best.

Rölvaag in Norwegian Literature

When Rölvaag started writing, it looked as if Ager would be his superior in the novel as well. He alone among Norwegian-American writers had succeeded in getting a novel published in Norway: his *Kristus for Pilatus* ("Christ before Pilate") of 1910, wrote Rölvaag the year after, "has, artistically speaking, reached a peak which it will be difficult for the rest of us to attain."[21] Beginning with *Amerika-Breve* in 1912, Rölvaag gradually achieved status as the outstanding Norwegian-American writer. That he and Ager could still become and remain fast friends throughout life is a tribute to the characters of both men.

We have outlined some aspects of the Norwegian reception of *I De Dage*— and *Riket Grundlægges* in Chapter 9. Another bit of lavish praise came from the hand of the above-mentioned Hans Aanrud: "He pours out with generous hands his charming knowledge and sympathy for humanity" in "a great saga about the fantastic land-taking of our countrymen."[22] In his obituary, the critic Elster declared that "his contribution will endure and have lasting significance. No one who concerns himself with the history of Norwegian emigration can overlook his novels. But they will also endure by virtue of their artistic qualities, their narrative power, and their character study. He had both the perspective and the intimate knowledge; he did not let himself be misled by national prejudices, nor confused by wishes and illusions. He wrote truthfully and sincerely, but with great love." He was "a splendid story teller, a warm and wise narrator. His novel sequence was planned on a large scale and carried through with insight, honesty, and clarity. His greatest contribution is his depiction of the transformation of the Norwegian immigrant type to an American type."[23]

It took several years, however, for a full-scale biographical and critical study to appear in Norway. In 1962 Gudrun Hovde Gvåle published a doctoral dissertation based on research in the Rölvaag family archives in Northfield.[24] Here the subtitle correctly identifies him as "Norwegian and American"; its three major divisions deal with his life, his work on behalf of Norwegian culture in America, and his literary production. This thorough and well-written study ought to have been translated, so that it might be available to American researchers. One chapter has appeared as an introduction to a 1966 reprint of *Peder Victorious*.[25] Not surprisingly, the author is better informed on and more sympathetic with Rölvaag's Norwegian roots than with his gradual Americanization. As her reviewers pointed out, she may have taken Rölvaag's jeremiads on the immigrant's rootlessness too seriously.[26]

That Rölvaag is indeed accepted within the canon of modern Norwegian literature appears from the three and a half pages devoted to him in the latest multivolumed history, written by Per Amdam (and edited by Edvard Beyer, 1975).[27] Otherwise, Norwegian critical attention has been modest, including articles by the historian Orm Øverland[28] and the student of literature Aashild Sørheim Erlandsen.[29] For a long time, his books were available only in an emasculated schoolbook version. In connection with the sesquicentennial of Norwegian emigration to America, the Norwegian Book Club issued an attractive modernized edition of the tetralogy (1975).[30]

Since Rölvaag persisted in writing in Norwegian because as he put it, English "did not sing for him," and he could hope for only a small audience among his Norwegian-American countrymen, his first readership would have to be found in Norway. He put great effort into keeping up with the rapid development of the language from the more stilted Dano-Norwegian toward the spoken dialects. Even today, once revised into modern spelling, his style is vividly oral, in keeping with the democratization of Norwegian writing.[31] He limited his Americanisms as far as possible to the dialogue and kept them within reason (with some needed help from the publishers' editors). But the process that began with the translation of *Giants* between 1925 and 1927 proved burdensome to him. He complained that it was taking as long to do a translation as to write a new book.[32] In his last year, he said that hereafter he would try writing in English first, and in fact he did write his unfinished memoirs ("Romance of a Life") in that language.[33]

Rölvaag in American Literature

We have earlier discussed the enthusiasm with which *Giants in the Earth* was received by American readers and reviewers alike.[34] One could go on citing at length, not only the reviewers throughout the width and breadth of the country, but also the hundreds of fan letters from readers who expressed directly to the author their vivid experience of the new view of pioneer life he presented.[35] Popular response was followed by an interesting academic enthusiasm. Within two years, Harper's had published a low-priced school edition in their series, Harper's Modern Classics, with an introduction by the outstanding historian of American literature, Vernon L. Parrington.[36] By 1930 a still cheaper edition was put on the market by Burt Company, and in 1937 Blue Ribbon Books had published it. When paperbacks began appearing, it was at once issued in a series called Perennial Classics (1965). It appears to have been continuously in print since its first appearance, an unusual piece of evidence of how Americans have taken the book to their hearts.

It has also been widely anthologized. In 1940 (revised 1945) it was included in full in Harry Shaw's *A Complete Course in Freshman English*.[37] By 1949 this edition had sold 143,663 copies, the school editions 125,068, and the regular editions 120,552, making a total of very nearly 450,000 copies.[38] The book was widely used both in high school and college classes in English, there treated as an American classic.[39]

Early reviewers had before them Lincoln Colcord's introduction, with its glowing account of Rölvaag's life, as well as his evaluation of the book. Of serious academic critics, Vernon Parrington was the first to give it a place in American literature in his unfinished *Main Currents in American Thought* (1930).[40] He saw in the book evidence of "the growth of a maturer realism." For the first time, he suggested, settlement had been seen "in terms of emotion." It "penetrates to the secret inner life of men and women who undertook the heavy work of subduing the wilderness." Parrington saw it, as he says, "quite apart from all artistic values," as "a great historical document." He recognized that the cost of settlement had already been touched upon in the writings of Hamlin Garland and Willa Cather, who had pictured "despondent women" and showed "warm sympathy with the emotional life of pioneer women." But he felt that Rölvaag had probed more deeply, and that although the book stemmed "from a rich old-world literary tradition, it is at the same time deeply and vitally American."

Two of Rölvaag's colleagues at St. Olaf College, Theodore Jorgenson and Nora O. Solum, set to work soon after Rölvaag's death and, by 1939, were able to publish the first and so far the only reasonably complete biography of Rölvaag in English. This book is a veritable treasury of otherwise unavailable materials, such as translations of extracts from his diary, his letters, and other writings. However useful and admirable this compilation may be, it falls short of being either a critical or a readable work. The chronological scheme results in a good deal of repetitiousness, while minor details, overly lengthy quotations, and personal philosophizing follow upon one another, making it hard to gain an adequate perspective. The authors were perhaps too close to Rölvaag's life and times, and themselves too closely involved, for all their love and devotion to the subject.[41]

The only other book-length analysis in print is a modest volume by Paul Reigstad, who gives a charming and helpful overview of Rölvaag's life and work (1972). The emphasis is on *Giants in the Earth* and its art: he grants it the "stature of a minor classic." He makes extensive use of the author's letters, especially those in which he expresses esthetic judgments.

Over the years, a number of dissertations (master's as well as doctor's) have been written, mostly in English departments by persons who have known no Norwegian. Some of these, and the published articles that have been extracted from them, have offered valuable analyses of Rölvaag's work. We have cited some of them at appropriate points in this book, and list them in the bibliography. Symposia held at the foci of his life and work testify to a continued interest in further exploration: 1974 at St. Olaf College, 1976 at Dönna (when his bust was unveiled), 1978 at Augustana College.[42]

What might be called the American literary establishment has assigned him a place, usually within "immigrant" or "pioneer" literature. Carl C. Van Doren in *The American Novel* (1940) calls it "the best of all immigrant novels in the United States. . . . Completely naturalized, the book is as much a part of American literature as of Norwegian. . . . It is for all its profound realism, rich in matter and magical in style."[43] The critiques gathered in the *Library of Literary Criticism of Modern American Literature* (1969) are firmly united in assigning him to American literature.[44] Spiller's *Literary History of the United States* (4th edition, 1974) finds that Scandinavian-American literature "reached its highest point" in *Giants,* in which Rölvaag fulfilled his ambition "to become the spokesman of his people, to tell the story of the immigrant's part in the making of the great new nation."[45] Steensma (1962) goes so far as to find it "a sad reflection on American criticism" that he has been "given a back seat to such intellectual and artistic mediocrities as Dreiser, Farrell, Dos Passos, and in certain respects, Sinclair Lewis."[46]

Rivals and Successors

In a sense, all other Norwegian-American novelists were Rölvaag's rivals, especially Ager, but they were also part of the soil from which he grew.[47] His triumph left them in the shadow and to a large extent brought an end to the writing of literary Norwegian in America.

Bojer, the Norwegian novelist whose plans triggered Rölvaag's *Giants,* came to market in Norway a month later, but in English translation two years sooner. His book, *Vor Egen Stamme* (Our own stock, published in 1925 as *The Emigrants*), won plaudits and readers in both countries, but created no literary sensation.[48] A new book by Bojer had appeared in both countries at regular intervals, and there was a general tendency to dismiss him as popular and superficial. In view of Bojer's lack of experience with immigration as well as America, it is not surprising that he lacked the authenticity and the depth of Rölvaag. But he told a good yarn, choosing his group of emigrants from his own native community in Tröndelag and settling them on the North Dakota frontier in the 1880s. He lays stress on the conditions of poverty and class distinction that stimulated the emigrants to leave; he also sees their alienation in the new land. But his basic idea is rather to show the pity for Norway who lost them and the gain for America who won them.[49]

We can give space only to a few words here on the great epic of the much later novelist from Sweden, Vilhelm Moberg, whose novel *The Emigrants (Utvandrarna,* 1949) grew into a tetralogy and was magnificently filmed by Jan Troell in two films with Liv Ullman and Max von Sydow playing the leads.[50] Moberg was already an experienced and well-established novelist when he undertook to write the story of emigration from his native Småland.[51] His experience of emigration was vicarious, like Bojer's, and like him, he chose to begin with a large and varied gallery of characters to typify various aspects and causes of emigration. He placed his frontier in the Minnesota of 1850 in what did indeed become the largest and most "Swedish" rural settlement in America, now known as Chisago County.[52] He has admitted to his biographer Gunnar Eidevall that he had read both Bojer's and Rölvaag's stories, but his working out of the epic is entirely his own.[53] The most striking parallel, which can hardly be entirely coincidental, is the way he narrows down his tale to a study of one couple, Karl Oskar and Kristina Nilsson. They play roles similar to those of Per Hansa and Beret. On arrival in New York, Kristina bursts into tears to Karl Oskar's surprise: "She was thinking of the road behind them—he was thinking of the way ahead."[54] Just so Per Hansa says about Beret: "There are some people, I know now, who never should emigrate, because you see, they can't take pleasure in that which is to come—they simply can't see it!"[55]

Moberg's work belongs to a different tradition and a different generation than Rölvaag's. There are others one would like to consider, for instance, Sophus Keith Winther, whose three novels of Danes in Nebraska, written in English, illustrate what he himself in a thoughtful article has called "The Emigrant Theme."[56] Among Midwestern writers, there is Ruth Suckow, much admired by Rölvaag, Herbert Krause, who wrote of Germans, and Fred Manfred, who writes of Frisians. There was Norwegian-born Martha Ostenso, whose grim story of Icelanders, *Wild Geese,* was more widely read than *Giants*. Yet so far, at least, as shown by Flatin (1977) Rölvaag's masterpiece stands unsurpassed within the genre by its fusion of art and reality.[57]

Conclusion

Rölvaag's work has been called an "anomaly" in American literature, because he wrote about his new life in Norwegian: as if all American literature had to be in English![58] In our day it has been recognized that America has a "multiethnic" literature, much of it written in languages other than English.[59] In a recent study, Rölvaag was described as "a writer between two countries,"[60] but I would amend that to read "a writer *with* two countries," both of which he loved as a man can love both mother and wife. It is also a question whether the phrase "a divided heart" can be applied to him, as in Skårdal's insightful study of Scandinavian-American literature.[61] When his alter ego in *Amerika-Breve* asserts that "we have become strangers; strangers to those we left, and strangers to those we came to," it must be taken as an epigrammatic half-truth most applicable to the relatively recent immigrant.[62] His love for the rolling waves of Nordland was entirely compatible with his love for the waving grasses of the prairie. His loyalty to Norway was motivated by an intense desire to bring its values to America and to leaven the cultural aridity of the Great Plains with the sourdough of a thousand-year-old tradition.

The Norwegian-America in which he lived and did his work most of his life was a real world, which called on his talents and nourished, however frugally, his genius. Most Americans were and are, as was Lincoln Colcord, unaware of its existence, and are pleasantly shocked when they discover it. Colcord opened a channel between this world and mainstream America. Rölvaag created his own channel back to the homeland; he wished to be a bridge builder between his old and his new land. In one of his most remarkable articles, published in Norway in 1924 in the wake of *I De Dage—*, he noted with regret that "those out West" and "those back East" no longer understood one another.[63] On both sides of the Atlantic, he fought his gallant battle to promote understanding. He may have lost most of the skirmishes, but by his lifework he still won the war. His writings held up a mirror to the life of Norwegian-America, illuminating its reality for the enjoyment and understanding both of Norwegians "back East" and Americans "out West."

Abbreviations

BL   *Boat of Longing*
DSD   *Den Signede Dag*
Gvåle   Gudrun Hovde Gvåle, *O. E. Rölvaag* (1962)
JB   Jennie Berdahl [Rölvaag]
J-S   Jorgenson and Solum, *Ole Edvart Rölvaag* (1939)
LB   *Længselens Baat*
Mrs. R.   Mrs. (Jennie Berdahl) Rölvaag
My trans.   Translation by writer
NAHA   Norwegian-American Historical Association (both as publisher and as archive at St. Olaf College)
OER   Ole Edvart Rölvaag
PS   *Peder Seier*
PV   *Peder Victorious*
SSN   *Scandinavian Studies and Notes*
TFG   *Their Fathers' God*

NOTE: Norwegian ø is everywhere transcribed *ö* in agreement with Rölvaag's own usage in English. The letters *æ*, *ö* (*ø*), *å* are alphabetized *ae, oe, aa.*

Notes and References

Chapter One

1. J-S, p. 388; Gvåle, p. 149.
2. OER to Mrs. R. ca. February 18, 1928, in J-S, pp. 388–89 (in English; original not found in Rölvaag Collection [NAHA]).
3. For full accounts of OER's life, see J-S and Gvåle.
4. *Giants* (New York, 1927), p. 3. All references to Rölvaag's works are to their first editions.
5. In a sarcastic letter answering an "Americanizer" named P. J. Slettedahl (which OER translates "Mr. Levelvally"), he anglicized his own name as "Auley Edward Rolfsbay," *Reform*, February 25, 1919.
6. On Dönnes Manor and its proprietors, the Coldevin family, see Gvåle, p. 43; and more fully, Axel Coldevin, *Jordegods og Storgårder i Nord-Norge* (Trondheim: Brun, 1943), pp. 166–80.
7. OER to JB, September 22, 1904. (My trans.)
8. On the literacy of the household, see Gvåle, p. 51; on Cooper, see Colcord, introduction to *Giants,* p. xiii.
9. OER, "Romance of a Life." Extracts printed in J-S, pp. 1–11; also in *American Prefaces* 1 (1936):99–101.
10. Owen W. Jordahl, "Folkloristic Influences upon Rölvaag's Youth," *Western Folklore,* January 1975, pp. 1–15. The *Nisse* is a brownie, a Robin Goodfellow; the *Good People* are elves and fairies living underground. The *Hulder* is a siren-like wood nymph. The *Draug* is a creature sailing a half-boat in the storm, an omen of death to sailors.
11. OER to JB, September 22, 1904 (trans.).
12. J-S, p. 23; Gvåle, p. 59 expresses some doubt in view of the passage of three years before the uncle responded. OER has himself described the storm in "Billeder fra Nordland" (*Nord-Norge,* December 1917), pp. 2–6; cited in part in Gvåle, p. 58. See also Colcord's account, introduction to *Giants,* p. xxvii.
13. On July 14–16, 1980, I was hospitably received by the superintendent of schools, Jon Austad, and his wife. Austad accompanied me to Rölvaag to meet Trygve and Ole Rölvaag, nephews of Ole Edvart. For a charming account of a similar visit by Paul Reigstad, see "Journey to Rølvaag" *Norseman,* no. 3, 1967, pp. 56–59. OER himself gave a full

account of his last return in "Den Gamle Stua," *Decorah-Posten,* January 13, 1925, partly cited in J-S, pp. 13–14.

14. *Længselens Baat,* pp. 11–12; *Boat of Longing,* pp. 1–2; also in "Romance of a Life," cited in J-S, pp. 1–11 and 18–21.

15. This and the following quotations are from OER to JB, September 22, 1904 (trans.).

16. The story of Kristian Andersen's offer of a boat is dramatically told by Colcord, introduction to *Giants,* pp. xxvii–xxviii, as reported to him by Rölvaag.

17. On Norwegian emigration to America, see Theodore C. Blegen, *Norwegian Migration to America 1825–1860* (Northfield, Minn., 1931); Carlton C. Qualey, *Norwegian Settlement in the United States* (Northfield, Minn., 1938); Arlow W. Andersen, *The Norwegian-Americans* (Boston, 1975), pp. 171–73.

18. On Foss, see Gvåle, p. 52; Dorothy Burton Skårdal, *The Divided Heart: Scandinavian Immigrant Experiences through Literary Sources* (Lincoln, Nebr., 1974), p. 222.

19. OER to JB, October 8, 1904 (NAHA).

20. Quotations (my trans.) from original in NAHA; there are many citations in J-S, p. 26ff (Chapter 3), but the translations are unduly free, e.g., the words here cited are translated "It is done; it is done. I have left home." Mrs. Rölvaag has made a transcription, which we follow here; she has also translated it.

21. OER, "The Genesis of *Giants in the Earth,*" *Editor* 78 (August 6, 1927):81–85. On November 1, 1981, the state of South Dakota placed a historical marker near the spot; *Sioux City Journal,* November 2, 1981.

22. MS diary (NAHA), March 20, 1898 (trans.).

23. P. J. Reinertsen to J. N. Kildahl, July 30, 1901 (NAHA archive, my trans.); cited in J-S, p. 55.

24. His experiences as a salesman and teacher are detailed in *Amerika-Breve* (1912) as the experiences of Per Smevik.

25. MS diary (NAHA), March 20, 1898 (trans.). Emphasis on "thinking" added by this writer for clarity's sake.

26. MS in NAHA archives; summary of its contents in J-S, pp. 75–78; Gvåle, pp. 108–10, 290–92. Gvåle notes as his original contribution the parochial school scenes.

27. Roy W. Meyer, *The Middle Western Farm Novel in the Twentieth Century* (Lincoln, Nebr., 1965).

28. Colcord to Saxton, March 9, 1926 (NAHA); incompletely cited in J-S, pp. 366–67.

29. There is adequate evidence that he did not swear in his home (personal communication from his daughter Ella V. Tweet) nor among his

colleagues. The profanity in his writing became something of an issue; see below.

30. Colcord, ibid. n. 28.

31. Clipping from Oslo newspaper, November 1931. The undated clipping leaves one without a clue to the identity of the recipient.

32. J-S, p.430.

Chapter Two

1. For the story of King Olaf (or Olav), see any history of Norway, e.g., Karen Larsen, *A History of Norway* (NY: Princeton U Press for the American-Scandinavian Foundation, 1948).

2. Oral reminiscence by Jorgenson in J-S, p. 140.

3. For a detailed history of St. Olaf College, see Joseph M. Shaw, *History of St. Olaf College 1874–1974* (Northfield, Minn., 1974).

4. In "Kildahl ved St. Olaf," ed. R. Malmin (Minneapolis: Augsburg, 1921), here cited from Gvåle, p. 97.

5. On the history of the Lutheran Church among the Norwegians, see E. Clifford Nelson and Eugene L. Fevold, *The Lutheran Church among Norwegians*, 2 vols. (Minneapolis, 1960).

6. Rölvaag, *Omkring Fædrearven* (Northfield, Minn., 1922), p. 82; on Nordgaard, see Gvåle, p. 91; and on Eikeland, see Gvåle, p. 98; also Shaw, *St. Olaf College,* p. 150.

7. Note the parallel: both Nordgaard and Eikeland had studied in Norway, and Rölvaag did the same.

8. Johannes B. Wist, *Norsk-Amerikanernes Festskrift* (Decorah, Iowa: the Symtra Company, 1914), pp. 112–14.

9. Gvåle (1962) gives a detailed account of the nationalistic currents in Norway in the late nineteenth century in her first chapter.

10. For further discussion of Bruun's ideas, see below, p. 39, with n. 18.

11. J-S (1939), p. 57; see also p. 218; and Shaw, *St. Olaf College,* p. 150.

12. Rölvaag, memorial to Eikeland (1927), here cited from Gvåle, p. 98; original not located.

13. Rölvaag to Mrs. R., June 23, 1910; here cited from J-S, p. 135.

14. Rölvaag, *Dr. John Nathan Kildahl: En Mindebok,* ed. R. Malmin (Minneapolis, 1921); here cited from Shaw, *St. Olaf College,* p. 174.

15. Rölvaag to Jennie Berdahl, May 20, 1908; here cited from J-S, p. 110. They (J-S) also suggested the benefit to Rölvaag of doing the glossary, p. 126.

16. Rölvaag to Farseth, July 15, 1912, here cited from J-S, p. 174.

17. Rölvaag to Farseth, January 8, 1908; here cited from Gvåle, p. 189; my trans., cf. J-S, p. 122.

18. Rölvaag, "Hvor Staar Vi Idag Med Hensyn Til Norsken," *Skandinaven*, May 24, 1911 (NAHA).

19. Ibid.

20. *Norsk Grammatik med Eksempler og Opgaver* (1st ed., Kristiania, Norway: Aschehoug, 1908; 2d ed., Minneapolis: Augsburg, 1917).

21. *Beginners' Book in Norse* (1910) and *Second Book in Norse* (1912), both published by Augsburg in Minneapolis.

22. Rölvaag, *Ordforklaring* (Minneapolis, 1909). The Norwegian reader was Nordahl Rolfsen, *Læsebok for Folkeskolen*, vol. 2 (Kristiania, 1908).

23. Rölvaag to Mrs. Rölvaag, June 23, 1910; here cited from J-S, p. 135.

24. *Haandbok* (Minneapolis, 1916).

25. On Norwegian spelling reforms, see Einar Haugen, *Language Conflict and Language Planning: The Case of Modern Norwegian* (Cambridge, Mass., 1966); on American textbooks in Norwegian, see Einar Haugen, *The Norwegian Language in America: A Study in Bilingual Behavior*, 2 vols. (Philadelphia, 1953), pp. 137–40 and ff. The new Norwegian editions are published by Den Norske Bokklubben (1975–77).

26. *Norsk Læsebok 2*, Forord; my trans.

27. *Manitou Messenger* (St. Olaf College), December 13, 1927.

28. Rölvaag to JB, January 18, 1908; here cited from J-S, p. 123.

29. *Manitou Messenger*, December 13, 1927.

30. Beginning with a series of six correspondences in *Skandinaven* (Chicago) in 1916, followed by three articles each in 1923 and 1925, finally in 1927, 1929, and 1930.

31. Spoken by President L. A. Vigness, according to Shaw, *St. Olaf College*, p. 175.

32. Mohn to F. B. Sanborn, November 28, 1888; here cited from Shaw, *St. Olaf College*, p. 240.

33. Ibid., p. 48.

34. For a thorough and unbiased view of the history of American legislation concerning language, see Heinz Kloss, *The American Bilingual Tradition* (Rowley, Mass.: Newbury House Publishers, 1969). For Norwegians, see Carl H. Chrislock, *Ethnicity Challenged: The Upper Midwest Norwegian-American Experience in World War I* (Northfield, Minn., 1981).

35. Clarence Kilde, "My Memories of Ole Edvart Rölvaag as a Teacher," unpublished manuscript (with the kind permission of the author).

36. Ella Valborg Rölvaag Tweet, "Recollections of My Father, O. E. Rölvaag," *Minnesota English Journal* 8 (1972):4–16.

37. Kilde, "Memories." In this case, the prophecy was more than fulfilled.

38. L. A. Vigness's administration intervened (1914–18), but left little impression on Rölvaag. For a warm and intimate account of Boe, see Erik Hetle, *Lars W. Boe, a Biography* (Minneapolis, 1949).

39. Rölvaag to Farseth, n.d.; here cited from J-S, p. 123.

40. Cited from a typed copy in the NAHA archives. (My trans.)

41. Shaw, *St. Olaf College,* p. 396.

42. Typed copy of draft in NAHA archives, in English.

43. Rölvaag to Kristine Haugen, December 20, 1923. In possession of author. (My trans.) See also his eloquent appeal in the papers, e.g., *Reform,* November 29, 1923: "Fram, Fram, Kristmænd, Korsmænd, Kongsmænd!"

44. On the complications involved, see Theodore Jorgenson, *Banner* (Northfield), no. 1, n.d.; and Shaw, *St. Olaf College,* p. 348.

Chapter Three

1. Early sociological uses of the term are in articles by E. K. Francis, "The Nature of the Ethnic Group," *American Journal of Sociology* 52 (March 1947):393–400, and "The Russian Mennonites: From Religious to Ethnic Group," *American Journal of Sociology* 54 (1948):101–7. For a recent assessment, see James H. Dorman, "Ethnic Groups and 'Ethnicity': Some Theoretical Considerations," *Journal of Ethnic Studies* 7 (1979–80):23–36, with a valuable bibliography.

2. By Peter A. Munch, sociologist; by a *lapsus calami,* he has placed Rölvaag in North instead of South Dakota.

3. In Joseph Hraba, *American Ethnicity* (Itasca, Ill.: Peacock, 1979), p. 27.

4. The writer was using this term before becoming aware that it is the title of a book by Howard F. Stein and Robert F. Hill (University Park: Pennsylvania State University Press, 1977).

5. A translation by Ella V. Tweet and Solveig Zempel appeared in 1971 entitled *The Third Life of Per Smevik.*

6. The preface is not included in the 1971 translation, though its contents are summarized in the introduction.

7. An obvious, unintentional misdating of the letter for May 23, 1899, as "1898" was overlooked by J-S, p. 148; all the later letters must be changed accordingly, as has been done in the translation. *Nykommerbreve,* references hereafter to pages in 1912 edition.

8. My trans.; the melodious line in the original ("Rullar ho, baara, so breid og blank millom landi") has not been identified (it may be by Rölvaag, though it is not in his usual language).

9. For a contrast, see Vilhelm Moberg, *The Emigrants* (New York: Simon and Schuster, 1951), Part Two, "Peasants at Sea," also below, Chapter 11, notes 50, 51.

10. Personal communication, Ella Valborg Tweet.

11. In letter to Fred Engene, cited here from J-S, p. 146; see also *The Third Life of Per Smevik* (trans. Tweet and Zempel), p. xx.

12. Søren Kierkegaard, *Either-Or,* trans. David F. Swenson and Lillian M. Swenson (N.Y.: Garden City, 1959), p. 1.

13. J-S, p. 156.

14. In *Dakota Farmer's Leader* (Canton, S.D.), June 7, 1901.

15. The speech (pp. 160–74) was translated under the title "Country and Fatherland" by Ellen and Eli Lewison in *American Prefaces* 1 (1936):109–12.

16. Robert Park, "Human Migration and the Marginal Man," *American Journal of Sociology* 33 (May 1928):881–93; Everett Stonequist, *The Marginal Man: A Study in Personality and Culture Conflict* (New York: Scribner, 1937).

17. See Neil Eckstein, "O. E. Rölvaag: The Marginality of the Bicultural Writer," in *Ole Rölvaag,* ed. Gerald Thorsen (Northfield, Minn., 1975), pp. 65–68.

18. Ibid., p. 66.

19. See Ray A. Billington, ed., *Frontier and Section: Selected Essays of Frederick Jackson Turner* (Englewood Cliffs, N.J.: Prentice-Hall, 1961).

20. Harold P. Simonson, *The Closed Frontier: Studies in American Literary Tragedy* (New York, 1970), p. 6.

21. Note by Mrs. Rölvaag, Box 41, NAHA archives.

22. Anthony Burgess, in *Encyclopædia Britannica* (15th ed., 1974), *Macropædia,* vol. 13, p. 287.

23. Phrases taken from reviews by L.P. Thorkveen (*Lutheraneren* ca. December 16, 1912); Anon. (*Lutheraneren,* June 11, 1912); Henrik Voldal (place not identified); O. L. Kirkeberg (place not identified); Anon. (*Kvartalskrift,* January 1913); in Scrapbook 36, Rölvaag Collection, NAHA.

24. *Decorah-Posten,* November 9, 1912.

25. Prestgard understood and commented on the central problem of the book, contrary to J-S, p. 166. Per Smevik refers to himself as twenty-three years old; this checks with Rölvaag's chronology, although the letter is misdated 1898, as noted above, n. 7.

26. Johan Rölvaag to OER, January 25, 1913; in Rölvaag Collection, NAHA; my trans.

27. OER to O. C. Farseth, March 9, 1913, here cited and translated from Gvåle, p. 299.

Chapter Four

1. An English translation in manuscript form is available in the Rölvaag collection, NAHA, by Mrs. C. F. Nickerson.

2. *Dagbog,* July 29, 1896. All quotations from the diary are translated from the transcription of the original made by Mrs. Rölvaag and deposited in the collection at NAHA. The original, which is also there, has been randomly checked.

3. *Dagbog,* August 1, 1896.

4. *Dagbog,* August 17–18, 1896.

5. *Dagbog,* January 2, 1899 (Augustana); this was Bertha Helseth of Sioux City, Iowa, who died soon after of tuberculosis.

6. *Dagbog,* June 10, 1900; this was Bessie Lappegaard of Canton, S.D. He learns of the rejection, *Dagbog,* November 30, 1900.

7. P. J. Reinertsen to J. N. Kildahl, July 30, 1901; in Rölvaag Collection, NAHA.

8. OER to JB, August 3, 1905 (J-S, p. 87).

9. OER to JB, May 20, 1908 (J-S, p. 110).

10. "It is impossible to discuss the main factors in Rölvaag's life and authorship without giving a prominent place to his religion." In Theodore Jorgenson, *Norwegian-American Studies and Records* 10 (1938):140.

11. *Paa Glemte Veie* (On forgotten paths) (Minneapolis, 1914), p. 10; hereafter page references cited in the text.

12. Above, p. 29, and n. 14.

13. For the Norwegian background of Norwegian-American Lutheranism, see Nelson and Fevold, *The Lutheran Church.*

14. On Lutheranism generally, see articles in the *Encyclopædia Britannica* (1974), vol. 11, s.v. "Lutheran Churches" by R. P. Scharlemann.

15. On Hauge, see Nelson and Fevold, *The Lutheran Church,* 1:13–23 and passim. In 1926 Rölvaag (with M. O. Wee) edited a volume in memory of Hauge's centennial (d. 1824), with an important preface, saying, e.g., "Is it not the implacable integrity of a Hauge that we need?"

16. On Grundtvig's influence in Norway, see Nelson and Fevold, *The Lutheran Church,* 1:27.

17. Kierkegaard is not mentioned in Nelson and Fevold; his influence was more literary than churchly and can be studied in any history of Norwegian literature or in a biography of Ibsen.

18. *Folkelige Grundtanker* (roughly translated as "a philosophy for the people") became a kind of bible for the populistic movements in nineteenth-century Norway. Rölvaag mentions Bruun and cites him in his commencement speech at St. Olaf on "Individuality."

19. Harold P. Simonson, "Rölvaag and Kierkegaard," *Scandinavian Studies* 49 (1977):67–80.

20. From Rölvaag's lecture notes in his Ibsen course, as quoted in J-S, p. 273.

21. *Decorah-Posten,* May 7, 1915.

22. *Lutheraneren,* n.d. (Rölvaag Scrapbook, NAHA).

23. E. Kr. Johnsen, *Lutheraneren,* n.d. (Scrapbook).

24. Jon Norstog, n.d., n.p. (Scrapbook).

25. *Reform,* December 22, 1914. Ager is also unhappy about Rölvaag's dialectal and Americanized diction.

26. Waldemar Ager, "Ole Edvard Rölvaag," in *Fortællinger og Skildringer* (Minneapolis, [1932]), p. 11.

Chapter Five

1. On the campaigns against foreign languages, see Kloss, *The American Bilingual Tradition* (Rowley, Mass.: Newbury House, 1977), p. 52, etc.

2. As secretary he edited a page under this title in the newspaper *Visergutten* from February 3, 1921, to June 15, 1922. He also engaged in a controversy with the American Legion at Lake Mills, Iowa, when the society held its meeting there on July 4, 1921; the Legion felt that the national holiday would be desecrated by "public service" in a "foreign language." Rölvaag protested that in the Lake Mills area, Norwegian was not a "foreign" language (Rölvaag to John R. King, draft in NAHA).

3. Articles in *Lutheraneren,* December 11, 1918; October 12, 1919; April 30-May 14, 1919.

4. For a more detailed account of the name controversy, see Einar Haugen, *Norwegian Language in America* (Philadelphia, 1953), pp. 256–58, 275. An excellent recent study is Carl H. Chrislock, "Name Change and the Church 1918–1920," *Norwegian-American Studies* 27 (1977):194–223, esp. pp. 207–20.

5. Haugen, *Norwegian Language in America,* p. 257; Kloss, *American Bilingual Tradition,* p. 61.

6. *Lutheraneren,* December 11, 1918, p. 1497.

7. Only in the 1930 translation are the sections given captions.

8. *To Tullinger,* p. 18. Quotations are from the Norwegian original, my trans. Hereafter page references are cited in the text.

9. *Editor,* March 1, 1930, p. 165.

10. For an excellent analysis, see Charles Boewe, "Rölvaag's America: An Immigrant Novelist's Views," *Western Humanities Review* 11 (1957):3–12.

11. *To Tullinger,* p. 34.

12. Examples from Chapter 1 of *To Tullinger;* on American-Norwegian, see Haugen, *Norwegian Language in America,* esp. Chapter 5.

13. [N. N. Rönning], *Familiens Magasin,* June 1921.

14. OER to Lincoln Colcord, December 2, 1927 (NAHA).

15. Waldemar Ager, in *Reform,* January 4, 1921; the same in *Kvartalskrift,* 1920.

16. Simon Johnson, *Normanden* (Grand Forks, N.D.), December 18 (19?), 1920.

17. *Lutheraneren,* December 17, 1920, p. 1578.

18. Attacks by M. C. Holseth, *Skandinaven,* September 23, 1921; and Christen Saxlund, *Skandinaven,* July 29, 1925 [?]; replies by C. O. Christiansen and Alf Houkom, *Skandinaven,* n.d. [clippings in Rölvaag Scrapbooks].

19. OER to Saxton, June 21, 1929.

20. *To Tullinger* (1920); *Pure Gold* (1930); hereafter cited in the text.

21. OER to Saxton, June 29, 1929; also to Saxton, November 23, 1927: "The novel is rather bizarre, but as far as I know, there is nothing like it in American literature. The only book I could compare it with would be *The Scarlet Letter.*"

22. *Rent guld,* "Efterord," p. 303.

23. *Saturday Review* 6 (March 22, 1930):856.

24. *Press Guardian* (Paterson, N.J.), February 10, 1930.

25. *Daily News* (St. Paul, Minn.), February 9, 1930.

26. *News Sentinel* (Knoxville, Tenn.), April 13, 1930.

27. *New York Times,* February 9, 1930, p. 9.

28. *Books,* February 9, 1930, p. 6.

29. March 19, 1930; n.d.; February 8, 1930.

30. *Creative Reading* 4 (February 15, 1930):153–69.

31. Lincoln Colcord to OER, March 19, 1930.

32. *"Pure Gold:* An Appreciation," in *Ole Rölvaag,* ed. Thorsen, p. 31. See also Erling Larsen, "The Art of O. E. Rölvaag," *Minnesota English Journal* 8 (1972):17–29, esp. 20–22, where he suggests that Lizzie and Lars are "as much destroyed by their surrounding community as they are by themselves."

Chapter Six

1. The sections promised but never written are headed "At Dawn," "The Reunion," "The Great Abomination," and "The Boat of Longing." See note 43 below.

2. [Carl G. O. Hansen] in *Minneapolis Tidende,* February 9, 1933.

3. Gerald Sykes, "Keeping Up with the Novelists," *Bookman,* March 1933, p. 303.

4. From the Foreword. Most of the translations in this chapter are my own versions of the original with reference to *LB* (1921); citations from the Solum translation are marked *BL.* While the latter is excellent, it is often quite free. For the Ibsen reference, see Koht, *Life of Ibsen* (New York: Blom, 1971), p. 356 (letter to F. Hegel, September 2, 1884).

5. It does appear in the Foreword.

6. *BL* has replaced it with "The Cove under the Hill."

7. Chapter 3, p. 31. A valuable commentary on Rölvaag's Nordland and his use of it here is John Heitmann, "Ole Edvart Rölvaag," *Norwegian-American Studies and Records* 12 (1941):144–66.

8. From *LB*, 11 (*BL*, 1). Quotations in this chapter are placed in the notes to avoid having to list both original and translation in the text.

9. Phantom ships are well known, but usually as omens of shipwreck (Stith Thompson, *Motif Index*, E53513; Feilberg, *Ordbog*, 3:243).

10. *LB*, 43 (*BL*, 29).

11. *LB*, 72 (*BL*, 54).

12. *LB*, 78 (*BL*, 59).

13. *LB*, 94 (*BL*, 73–74).

14. *LB*, 100 (*BL*, 78).

15. Translated in *BL* as "In Foreign Waters."

16. Rölvaag mostly refers to him as "Poeten" (in quotation marks); although the name is German, he is Norwegian. It may be intended to suggest (ironically) that he is a would-be wise man. In the translation, it is spelled Weisman (*BL*, 103; *LB*, 131).

17. All the poems but one ("Astray," *BL*, 101) are rendered by Thomas Job, often very freely; Job, a professor at Carleton College, was the author of a dramatization of *Giants in the Earth*. (New York: Harper's, 1929). For further discussion, see below, Chapter 11, p. 112–15.

18. *LB*, 179 (*BL*, 146).

19. *LB*, 143 (*BL*, 115).

20. *LB*, 144 (*BL*, 115); here the phantom boat is named for the first time, giving both the tune and the book their names.

21. Translated as "Adrift."

22. *BL*, 243 (*LB*, 296).

23. Translated as "Hearts That Ache."

24. *LB*, 337 (*BL*, 276).

25. Byron in *Childe Harold*, Canto IV; Björnson, *Samlede Digter-verker* (1919), 8:223–26; Alexander Kielland, *Samlede Digter-verker* (1919), 1:87.

26. *LB*, 357 (*BL*, 294).

27. *BL*, 146 (*LB*, 179).

28. Matthew 16:26.

29. Ibsen, *Peer Gynt*, esp. acts 2 and 5.

30. Rölvaag, "Christian Doctrine in Ibsen's 'Peer Gynt,' " *Religion in Life* 1 (1932):70–89.

31. *LB*, 178 (*BL*, 145).

32. *LB*, 179 (*BL*, 146).

33. See Chapters 7 and 8 below.

34. Sverre Lyngstad, *Jonas Lie* (Boston: Twayne Publishers, 1977), p. 119.

35. J-S, p. 279.

36. Lyngstad, *Jonas Lie*, pp. 24–33.
37. On the *bygdelag* in general, see Odd S. Lovoll, *A Folk Epic: The Bygdelag in America* (Boston, 1975). He reports on the organization of Nordlandslaget, p. 61. Rölvaag's newspaper appeals on behalf of the society and its purposes are little masterpieces. For comment by his fellow Dönnaman, John Heitmann, see *Norwegian-American Studies and Records* 12 (1941):144–66.
38. See Carl G. O. Hansen, *My Minneapolis* (Minneapolis: by the author, 1956), p. 145ff.
39. Kristoffer F. Paulson, "Rölvaag as Prophet: The Tragedy of Americanization," in *Ole Rölvaag,* ed. Thorson, pp. 57–64.
40. *Nord-Norge,* no. 24 (1921); also in *Duluth Skandinav,* n.d. (clippings in Rölvaag papers, NAHA).
41. *Washington-Posten,* n.d. (clipping, NAHA).
42. *Familiens Magasin,* January 1923.
43. *Reform,* January 3, 1922. Rölvaag's close friend, John Heitmann of Duluth, reports on a post-*Giants* conversation in which he outlined a complete plan for revision of *Længselens Baat:* "Ager was right in his critique of the book, and it cannot be published in English in its present form." But he had not yet found the right form for the intended continuation. (*Decorah-Posten,* August 29, 1941.)
44. *Familiens Magasin,* January 1923.
45. Ibid.
46. *Nordmandsforbundet,* no. 1 (1922).
47. *Decorah-Posten,* n.d., 1921 (pseud. Arnljot).
48. *Skandinaven,* review dated December 16, 1921.
49. OER to Saxton, March 31, 1930 (NAHA).
50. *New York Times Book Review,* January 22, 1933, p. 6.
51. *New York Sun,* January 21, 1933.
52. *Bookman,* March 1933, pp. 302–3.
53. *New York Evening Post,* here cited from *Nordisk Tidende,* March 14, 1933.
54. For references to these studies, see the Bibliography.
55. *Catholic World* 137 (June 1933):379.
56. See discussion in Einar Haugen, "O. E. Rölvaag: Norwegian-American," *Norwegian-American Studies and Records* 7 (1933):53–73, esp. p. 62.

Chapter Seven

1. J-S, p. 221.
2. Communication, Ella Valborg Tweet.
3. The idea of a collection of Rölvaag letters was proposed as long ago as May 29, 1939, by Dean Theodore C. Blegen in a letter to Mrs.

Rölvaag, both as a biographical memorial and because he was "a masterful letter writer" (NAHA).

4. In the Rölvaag collection, NAHA.

5. OER to Farseth, January 7, 1906.

6. OER to Farseth, December 8, 1912.

7. OER to Farseth, March 9, 1913.

8. "Til Nordlændingerne," n.d. [1909] (Scrapbook, NAHA); "Nord-lands-Brev Til 'Nord-Norge,' " *Nord-Norge*, December 1916, pp. 18–20.

9. OER to Ruth Lima (McMahon), November 29, 1925; here cited from J-S, p. 379.

10. One of the most significant of his literary correspondents was his fellow writer, Simon Johnson. Their correspondence is the subject of a valuable study by Lloyd Hustvedt (1976), revealing all too clearly the difference between a "loser" and a "winner." See below, p. 71.

11. Rölvaag visited the Newburgers in their home at Coral Gables, near Miami, in the summer of 1931. He wrote an introduction to a collection of Newburger's poems, "Oriental Sketches and Other Themes." In this, he defined poetry as a "blend of mood and idea."

12. These letters were not available at that time.

13. Kristine Haugen (1878–1965), b. in Oppdal, m. J. Haugen 1904, made her home in Sioux City, Iowa; Signe Mydland Steinarson (1871–1928), b. in Sirdal, m. H. Steinarson 1912; Mimmi-Marie Halling Swensen (1877–1965), m. Johannes Swensen 1896, residing at Hildestad.

14. OER to Kristine Haugen, April 29, 1922 (in this writer's possession; photocopies in NAHA).

15. OER to Kristine Haugen, November 8, 1922.

16. OER to Kristine Haugen, July 12, 1923.

17. OER to Signe Mydland Steinarson, October 9, 1925.

18. OER to Signe Mydland Steinarson, n.d. [ca. September 1, 1926].

19. Rölvaag's letters to her (thirty-eight in all, obviously incomplete) are in Universitetsbiblioteket, Oslo, Brevsamling 543, except for the one cited below, note 25. They are used here by permission of her daughter, Else Halling, Oslo, and the Universitetsbibliotek, thanks to librarian Öivind Anker. A few of her letters are in the Rölvaag Papers, NAHA. These letters have not previously been identified.

20. Her review of *I De Dage*— appeared in *Holmestrands-posten*, November 1924; also her review of *Riket Grundlægges*, April 2, 1926.

21. Hildur Dixelius (1879–1969) was herself a minister's daughter; this novel appeared in Stockholm in 1920, the translation *Prestedatteren* in Kristiania in 1922, and an English translation, *The Minister's Daughter* (New York: Dutton, 1926).

22. OER to Mimmi Swensen, September 13, [1926].

23. OER to Mimmi Swensen, July 21, 1926.

24. OER to Mimmi Swensen, September 13, [1926].

25. OER to Mimmi Swensen, March 8, 1927 (in Rölvaag Papers, NAHA).

26. Ibid.

27. OER to Mimmi Swensen, Oslo, [March 13, 1928]. On her later life, see interview in *Kongsberg*, July 3, 1962.

28. For example, in the Bojer article cited below (*SSN* 9 [1926–27]:67.)

29. On these college book reviews, see J-S, pp. 63–64.

30. *Reform*, February 1, 1916 (review of poems by Baumann).

31. *Decorah-Posten*, January 9, 1917.

32. *Kvartalskrift*, 1920.

33. *Duluth Skandinav*, February 27, 1925.

34. *Skandinaven*, July 10, 1925.

35. OER to Kristine Haugen, September 2, 1925.

36. *Gamlelandets Sönner*, reviewed in *Skandinaven*, November 20, 1926; *Hundeöine*, reviewed in *Norden*, January 1930. Rölvaag persuaded Harper's to publish an English translation of the latter, entitled *I Sit Alone* (1931). For a sympathetic review of Ager's work, see Kenneth Smemo, "The Norwegian Ethnic Experience and the Literature of Waldemar Ager," in *Norwegian Influence on the Upper Midwest*, ed. Harald Naess (Duluth, 1976), pp. 59–64.

37. Ibid.

38. This and other quotations in this paragraph are from Lloyd Hustvedt, "The Simon Johnson-Ole Edvart Rölvaag Correspondence," in *Norwegian Influence*, ed. Naess.

39. OER, "When a Novelist Is in a Hurry," *Scandinavian Studies and Notes* 9 (1926–27):61–67.

40. *Nordisk Tidende*, December 24, 1925.

41. *Norden* (Chicago), January 1929, p. 23.

42. Walter Vodges in *Nation*, July 13, 1927.

43. OER, "America Come to Europe," *New York Herald Tribune Books*, October 25, 1931.

44. "Omkring Sinclair Lewis og Nobelprisen," *Norden*, February 1931, pp. 4–5. This was the more generous, since Rölvaag's own name had been put in the running by friends.

45. Ibid.

46. J-S, p. 394; the manuscript is in NAHA.

47. *Omkring Fædrearven*, pp. 140–59; for partial translations, see J-S, pp. 310–16.

48. Contrary to J-S, p. 308, Rölvaag does mention *Paa Glemte Veie* in his list, see p. 130 ("om den daglige korsfæstelse").

49. *Omkring Fædrearven*, p. 140.

50. Ibid., p. 144.

51. Rumor has it that an English version is in preparation.

Chapter Eight

1. *Giants in the Earth: A Saga of the Prairie*, trans. Lincoln Colcord and the Author (New York and London, 1927), p. 21; hereafter page references cited in the text.

2. *Giants*, p. 110; here translated from the original, p. 101.

3. Carroll D. Laverty, "Rölvaag's Creation of the Sense of Doom in *Giants in the Earth*," *South Central Bulletin* 27, no. 4 (1967):45.

4. See Harald Beyer, *History of Norwegian Literature* (New York: New York University Press, 1956), esp. pp. 290–313; also biographies in *Columbia Dictionary of Modern European Literature*, 2d ed. (New York: Columbia University Press, 1980), pp. 677–78.

5. Harry Salpeter, interview with Rölvaag, *New York World*, February 26, 1928.

6. Alfred Hauge, *Cleng Peerson*, 2 vols., trans. Erik Friis (Boston: Twayne Publishers, 1975).

7. Vilhelm Moberg, *The Emigrants*, 4 vols., trans. Gustaf Lannestock (New York: Simon & Schuster, 1951).

8. Johan Bojer, *The Emigrants*, trans. A. G. Jayne (New York: Appleton-Century, 1934).

9. In 1979, the house in which Rölvaag and Jennie Berdahl were married and spent their honeymoon was removed to the campus of Augustana College in Sioux Falls and dedicated as the Berdahl-Rölvaag House, after restoration by the Nordland Heritage Foundation.

10. O. E. Rölvaag, "The Genesis of *Giants in the Earth*," *Editor*, 78 (August 6, 1927):81–85.

11. Kristoffer F. Paulson, "Berdahl Family History and Rölvaag's Immigrant Trilogy," *Norwegian-American Studies* 27 (1977):55–76.

12. See below, ch. 10, n. 37.

13. OER to Andreas and Per Rölvaag, November 8, 1925 (copy by Mrs. OER, 1933, in NAHA).

14. Le Roy G. Davis, "The Study of Pioneer Life: A Communication," *Minnesota History* 10 (1929):430–35.

15. Einar Hoidale, "The Study of Pioneer Life: Two Replies to Mr. Davis," *Minnesota History* 11 (1930):63–74: letters from Einar Hoidale (January 24, 1930) and J. H. Klovstad (January 3, 1930).

16. For an earlier and more detailed account of the myths, see this writer's Introduction to the Torchbook edition of *Giants* (New York: Harper's, 1964), pp. ix–xxiii.

17. Hjalmar Rued Holand, *De Norske Settlementers Historie* (Ephraim, Wisc.: by the author, 1908), pp. 502–6. Called to my attention by Kurt

Larson, University of Minnesota. Translated as *Norwegians in America* by H. M. Blegen (Sioux Falls, S.D., Heritage Foundation, 1978).

18. Ibid., pp. 502–3. My trans.

Chapter Nine

1. Hutchison writes: "For this Norse teller of tales, this saga-maker, there were giants within the earth, the stubborn glebe." (*New York Times*, May 29, 1927, p. 5). In the Rölvaag papers, there is a letter to Nora Solum from a director of extension in a Texas college asking her to settle for his class whether the "giants" are "the great forces of loneliness" or "the heroic settlers themselves." Unfortunately, her answer is not extant, but I believe the answer is the one given here.

2. *Omkring Fædrearven*, p. 16.

3. For the story of Soria Moria Castle, see Asbjørnsen and Moe, *Norwegian Folk Tales*, available in various editions, e.g., trans. Pat Shaw Iversen and Carl Norman (New York: Viking Press, 1960), pp. 67–76. Other Ashlad stories are on pp. 17, 20, 77, 81, 170.

4. The text of available editions has *princess* here for *princes*; this is clearly a misprint, since the original has *prinser* ("princes"). In the Perennial Classic edition of *Giants*, this is on p. 45.

5. *Hansa* and *Olsa* are Nordland dialectal forms for the usual Norwegian *Hansen* and *Olsen*, patronymics which most immigrants adopted for ease of pronunciation. In rural Norway, the names in *-sen* were still patronymics; but in the second half of the nineteenth century, it became more common to adopt farm names, as being more distinctive and national. For a discussion, see Haugen, *Norwegian Language in America*, chapter 9.

6. J-S, p. 252. As quoted, apparently from Jorgenson's memory, Rölvaag also said: "I think it changed my entire view of life. Prior to May 18, 1920, I had looked upon God as a logical mind in Whom the least happening in this and in all other worlds was planned and willed. Gradually I began to see that much of what takes place is due to chance and to lawbound nature."

7. Ibid., p. 349. This passage exemplifies the expansion in the English version. In the original, the passage consists of only one sentence: "The Great Plain lay there, stretching itself in all its majesty. . . ." Note that the dots here do not represent omissions, but "thought pauses"; in the original, they are dashes. For the Norwegian passage, see *Riket Grundlægges*, p. 96.

8. Above, p. 66. See also Abraham Burstin, "Is the Jewish Problem of Survival Unique? An Interview with Prof. O. E. Rölvaag," *United Synagogue Recorder* 1929 (April):4–5.

9. The last sentence of this apostrophe was added in the English version to increase its meaningfulness to American readers.

10. Brand's words (Act 1) are: "Help is worthless to a man / who would not do more than he can." In a study of "Rölvaag and Kierkegaard," Harold P. Simonson points out that "the underlying issue is salvation, and Per Hansa is as far from it at the end of the novel as he was at the beginning." (*Scandinavian Studies* 49 (1977):69).

11. Maynard Fox, "The Bearded Face Set toward the Sun," *Ball State Teacher's College Forum* 1 (1961):62–64: "In fact, the tragedy of Per Hansa lies in the *sole* concentration of his energies upon a single and powerful end: the creation of the material symbols of his productivity" (64). Raychel Haugrud [Reiff], "In Quest of Soria Moria," Ph.D. dissertation, University of Utah, 1971, p. 93: "Therein lies his tragedy: he has neglected to develop his capacity to understand and sympathize with others, thinking solely of his need for self-realization."

12. See John Helgeland, "Beret's Problem: An Essay on Immigrant Pioneer Religion," *Lutheran Quarterly* 28 (1976):45–53.

13. The additions are on pp. 451–52 and 454–55, chapter 7, section 4 of Book 2, beginning, "All through the latter part of last summer" to "a child that is so delicate as she, he thought"; and from "Beret looked at the door" to "her sad mood did not lift." Also on p. 459, his oath.

14. Sidney Goldstein, "The Death of Per Hansa," *English Journal* (1969):464–66. Having nothing more to live for, he became one of those who "lay down and died" (*Giants*, p. 424).

15. Joseph E. Baker, "Western Man Against Nature: *Giants in the Earth*," *College English* 4 (1942):19. Rölvaag's own defense is found in a letter to Stavnheim, who had questioned it on first reading. As the chief psychological factors, he lists Per's friendship for Hans, Beret's inhuman religion, and Per's uncontrollable anger. (OER to Stavnheim, November 17, 1925).

16. *Aftenposten*, November 8, 1924.

17. C. J. Hambro, *Morgenbladet*, November 17, 1924. Inge Debes in *Nationen* (November 10, 1924) writes: Rölvaag is "a fully mature artist" and his book "is the work of a true poet."

18. Jørgen Bukdahl, "Emigranternes Saga," *Politiken*, June 17, 1929; see also his essay, *"Riget Grundlægges*: O. E. Rölvaag," in *Det skjulte Norge* (Copenhagen: Aschehoug, 1926), pp. 232–47.

19. Anon., "As Prophet Abroad: Norway Extols St. Olaf Man," *Minneapolis Journal*, January 31, 1926.

20. On Colcord, see *Who Was Who 1943–1950*; on his political role in 1917–18, see John E. Reinertson, "Colonel House, Woodrow Wilson, and European Socialism 1917–1919." Ph.D. Diss., University of Wisconsin, 1970, ch. 4 and 9.

21. A beginning has been made in an unpublished paper by Betty Bergland, who describes the relationship between the men as revealed in their letters; it went far beyond a purely professional friendship.

22. In the Rölvaag papers, there is a draft "Concerning the Translation of *Giants in the Earth*," originally composed by Colcord and revised by Rölvaag, intended to appear under the latter's name in *Saturday Review of Literature*. It does not seem to have appeared.

23. "Foreword," *Giants in the Earth* (1929 edition), p. x.

24. Introduction to *Giants in the Earth*, p. xi.

25. *Nation* 125 (July 13, 1927):41.

26. *Boston Transcript*, August 13, 1927, p. 4.

27. *Atlantic*, September 1927.

28. *Saturday Review of Literature* 3 (June 11, 1927):896.

29. "A European-American Genius," *Independent* 119 (July 9, 1927):44.

30. "Norwegian Pioneers in the Dakotas," *New York Times*, May 29, 1927, p. 5.

31. Walter Vodges, "Hamsun's Rival," *Nation*, July 13, 1927, p. 41.

32. *American Magazine*, October 1929, pp. 44–47, 83, 86.

33. *Decorah-Posten*, editorial, [May ?] 1927. See also review by Waldemar Ager in *Reform*, November 5, 1925; and the most thorough treatment of the whole series by Georg Strandvold, "Rölvaags Præriesaga," *Decorah-Posten*, December 11, 1931, to January 29, 1932. Also Olaf Holen, "Riget Grundlægges," *Skandinaven*, n.d.

34. *American-Scandinavian Review* 15 (1927):498.

35. As early as 1924, the historian and theologian O. M. Norlie attacked *I De Dage*— "for parading the 57 varieties of Norwegian swearing." (Norlie to OER, December 12, 1924). In 1927, N. N. Rönning attacked it in his papers *Familiens Magasin* and the *Friend* under the heading "A Book that should not be Recommended to Christian Youth," one of the unfit passages being the allusion to human and bovine lust. In 1930, the Reverend C. K. Solberg attacked the English translation of *Pure Gold* for its "frequent oaths and obscenities" and accused Rölvaag of misrepresenting the American-Norwegians, "befouling his own nest." (*Lutheraneren*, March 1930). After his death, a theological professor, G. M. Bruce, gave a lecture to a Norwegian literary society in Minneapolis in which he regretted that Norwegians for all time to come would be represented by such caricatures and "paper beings" as Per Hansa and Beret (*Minneapolis Tidende*, March 17, 1932).

36. Each of these attacks was vigorously refuted by Rölvaag's admirers. Most important was President Boe's stand, e.g., in a letter to Rölvaag of March 20, 1930: "Under no circumstances do I want you to take criticism

to heart to such an extent that you must resign. It would take the heart right out of me, because I would feel like resigning myself."

37. OER to Lars W. Boe, from Biloxi, Mississippi, March 23, 1930.

38. List taken from bibliography by Robert Bjerke, unpublished manuscript. The *Index Translationum* (1962) shows that versions have also appeared in Tamil (1960), Telugu (1961), and Hindi (1962).

39. Quotations, each from a different reviewer, from a publisher's blurb prepared for the German version, *Das Schweigen der Prairie* (Rölvaag papers, NAHA).

Chapter Ten

1. OER to Colcord, October 19, 1927 (NAHA). In an undated but post-*Giants* conversation with John Heitmann (of Duluth), he spoke of three novels plus a revision of *Længselens Baat* (*Decorah-Posten*, August 29, 1941); see above p. 61, with n. 43.

2. Solum was professor of English and Rölvaag's colleague at St. Olaf. Interesting letters from Ager to Rölvaag are in the collection of NAHA.

3. Translator's Foreword to *Their Father's God*, pp. v–vi.

4. *TFG*, 282–83; *DSD*, 262. Page references to the two novels and their translations will hereafter be abbreviated: *PV* (*Peder Victorious*), *PS* (*Peder Seier*), *DSD* (*Den Signede Dag*), *TFG* (*Their Father's God*). They will appear as notes, not in the main text.

5. *PV*, 319–20; *PS*, 361.

6. *PV*, 1–3; *PS*, 1–3.

7. *PV*, 32; *PS*, 39.

8. Translated from *PS*, 169; cf. *PV*, 142. Probably from a McGuffey Reader, although I have been unable to locate it.

9. *PV*, 169; *PS*, 200.

10. Translated from *PS*, 211; cf. *PV*, 179.

11. On loanwords in American-Norwegian, see Haugen, *The Norwegian Language in America*.

12. OER to Colcord, July 20, 1927; here cited from J-S, p. 380.

13. OER to Boynton, June 3, 1929.

14. Extracts from this letter were used by Boynton in his discussion of Rölvaag in *Literature and American Life* (Boston: Ginn, 1936), p. 842; parts of it were printed under Rölvaag's name in the Dallas (Texas) *Times Herald* (undated clipping, NAHA).

15. Ibid.

16. On Grundtvig, see above, p. 39, n. 16. The first line of the hymn runs: "The Blessed Day which now we see / with joyful promise dawning."

17. *TFG*, 94; *DSD*, 86.

18. *TFG*, 120; *DSD*, 111.

19. *TFG*, 153; *DSD*, 142.

20. See above, p. 4.

21. Paraphrased from *DSD*, 145; *TFG*, 156.

22. *TFG*, 157; *DSD*, 145.

23. *TFG*, 156; *DSD*, 145.

24. *TFG*, 158; *DSD*, 146.

25. *TFG*, 314; *DSD*, 291.

26. *TFG*, 315; *DSD*, 292.

27. *TFG*, 318; *DSD*, 295.

28. For example, in a letter from President Boe to C. F. Berg, December 7, 1931: "It was Rölvaag's plan to write a fourth book of this series and he time and again said, 'Beret is coming back in her boy.' " (NAHA).

29. As Rölvaag undoubtedly knew, the election of 1896 saw a contest between two men of Norwegian birth for the governorship, the winning Populist candidate Andrew Lee, and the losing Republican candidate Amund Ringsrud. See Roald Steen "Da guvernørvalget sto mallom to nordmenn," *Nordmanns-Forbundet* (No. 6, 1981), pp. 202–3.

30. *TFG*, 207; *DSD*, 188.

31. *TFG*, 209; *DSD*, 190.

32. *TFG*, 210; *DSD*, 191.

33. *TFG*, 253; *DSD*, 233 (where it says only, "in our family").

34. *TFG*, 260; *DSD*, 240.

35. *TFG*, 264; *DSD*, 244.

36. Translated from *DSD*, 314; *TFG*, 338.

37. *Progress Magazine*, undated clipping, citing Dana R. Bailey, *History of Minnehaha County* (Sioux Falls, S.D., 1899), pp. 254–57. Clipping in Rölvaag Collection (NAHA), which Rölvaag must have seen.

38. OER to Ruth Lima (McMahon), November 29, 1925; here cited from J-S, p. 379. See above, p. 66.

39. Interview by Sigfred and Roe in *Northfield News*, October 9, 1931. Regulations for voting were looser in those days; Rölvaag's boss made the arrangements.

40. Interview in Minneapolis, June 15, 1981.

41. OER to Mrs. R., January 15, 1931.

42. L. W. Boe to C. F. Berg, December 7, 1931.

43. *New York Herald Tribune Books*, October 18, 1931, p. 7.

44. Anon., December 30, 1931, p. 2.

45. Anon., January 27, 1932, p. 122.

46. Anon., October 31, 1931.

47. Fred T. Marsh, "Clashing Loyalties," *New York Sun*, October 23, 1931.

48. Anon., November 1, 1931, p. 6.

49. N. Glazer and D. P. Moynihan, *Beyond the Melting Pot* (Cambridge, Mass.: M.I.T. Press, 1963).

50. Figures from Frances L. Tyler, "O. E. Rölvaag: His Place in American Literature," M.A. thesis, University of Missouri, 1950, p. 144.

51. Clifton Fadiman, Review of *Peder Victorious, Forum* 81 (March 1929):xx, xxi.

52. Gvåle, p. 396.

Chapter Eleven

1. For example, in the letter to Mimmi Swensen cited above, p. 68, n. 24.

2. Kenneth Bjork, "The Unknown Rölvaag," *Norwegian-American Studies and Records* 11 (1940):122.

3. On Blegen's work as a historian of immigration, see Carlton C. Qualey's tribute in *Norwegian-American Studies* 21 (1962):3–13, with bibliography.

4. See note 2.

5. Above p. 56, note 17.

6. *LB*, 128; *BL*, 100.

7. For *Arne*, see B. Björnson, *Samlede Digter-Verker*, ed. Francis Bull (1919) 1:335–433; there are ten poems, most of them attributed to Arne himself.

8. *LB*, 167; *BL*, 135; in Job's version, "The Ballad of Soria Moria."

9. In the Rölvaag Collection (NAHA), there is an alphabetical list by Mrs. Rölvaag.

10. A long narrative poem, unfinished, appears to have been intended as one of a cycle about "Ola-gutten" (i.e., himself) reminiscent of A. O. Vinje's *Storegut*.

11. *LB*, 167; *BL*, 135.

12. Rölvaag Collection (NAHA).

13. *LB*, 248; *BL*, 203.

14. "Stemninger Fra Prærien," *Jul i Vesterheimen*, 1912; reprinted in *Norsk Læsebok* 1:193–202; *Fortællinger og Skildringer*, pp. 42–51.

15. Stories and sketches appeared in the issues for 1912, 1914, 1917, 1920 (a prose poem), 1921, 1925, 1928, and 1931.

16. "Hvitbjørn og Graabjørn, et Indiansk Eventyr," *Symra* (Decorah, Iowa) (1913):116–19; reprinted in *Deklamationsboken*, p. 299; *Fortællinger og Skildringer*, pp. 61–65.

17. "Naar sneen daler ved juletide, gammelt sagn," *Jul i Vesterheimen*, 1914; reprinted in *Deklamationsboken*, pp. 156–59; *Norsk Læsebok*, 2:177–80; *Norsk Ungdom* 18 (1930):182–83; *Fortællinger og Skildringer* (1932), pp. 27–29. Translated in *American Prefaces* 1 (April 1936):102–3, by Stanley Heggen.

18. "Klare Morgen og Vaate Kveld," *Jul i Vesterheimen*, 1921, reprinted in *Fortællinger og Skildringer*, pp. 66–83.

19. *Fortællinger og Skildringer* (Minneapolis: Augsburg, [1932]).

20. "Two Stories by O. E. Rölvaag with an Essay by Waldemar Ager," Senior honors thesis, St. Olaf College, May 1, 1969 [NAHA]. The stories are "Smörkrigen i Greenfield" (1928) and "Ogsaa et Juleoffer" (1931).

21. OER to Farseth, December 31, 1911; here cited from J-S, p. 144.

22. *Aftenposten* (Oslo), November 7, 1925; here cited from Gvåle, p. 366.

23. *Aftenposten* (Oslo), November (?) 1931.

24. Gvåle 1962, cf. Forord, pp. 9–10.

25. *Peder Victorious*, Introduction by Gudrun Hovde Gvåle, translated and adapted by Einar Haugen (New York: Harper & Row, a Perennial Classic, 1964).

26. The reviewers referred to were "opponents" at the doctoral disputation; their papers are printed in *Edda* (Oslo) 53 (1966). They were Sigmund Skard (pp. 361–80), Ingrid Semmingsen (pp. 381–98), and Dorothy Burton Skårdal (pp. 398–402).

27. *Norges Litteratur Historie* 4 (1975):363–66.

28. Orm Överland, "Ole Edvart Rölvaag and *Giants in the Earth:* A Writer between Two Countries," *American Studies in Scandinavia* 13 (1981):35–45; Överland, "Ole Edvart Rölvaag og den Norske Kulturen i Amerika," forthcoming.

29. Aashild Sørheim [Erlandsen], "To Fedreland Eller Intet?" Hovedoppgave til nordisk hovedfag, Universitetet i Oslo, 1977. (Copy at NAHA).

30. Den Norske Bokklubben. A note in each volume mentions that the text has been cautiously modernized. The changes are almost entirely orthographic.

31. On language development in Norway, see Haugen, *Language Conflict and Language Planning*.

32. OER to Nora Solum, January 11, 1931; here cited from Gvåle, p. 405.

33. In Rölvaag Collection, NAHA; for quotations, see J-S, pp. 1–11, 13–21.

34. Above, Chapter 9, pp. 94–96.

35. For a detailed study of a selection of 250 fan letters lent her by Mrs. Rölvaag, see Frances L. Tyler, "O. E. Rölvaag: His Place in American Literature," M.A. thesis, University of Missouri, 1950.

36. *Giants in the Earth*, with Introduction by Vernon L. Parrington, late professor of English, University of Washington, (New York, 1929), pp. ix–xx.

37. Harry Shaw, *A Complete Course in Freshman English* (New York: Harper's, 1940), pp. 538–839.

38. Figures from Tyler, "O. E. Rölvaag," pp. 144–45 (information from publisher).

39. Selections have also appeared in Jay B. Hubbell, ed., *American Life in Literature* (New York: Harper's, 1936), pp. 767–77; H. Warfel, R. Gabriel, and S. Williams, eds., *The American Mind* (New York: American Book Co., 1937), pp. 1402–12; and Maxine S. Seller, ed., *Immigrant Women* (Philadelphia: Temple University Press, 1981), pp. 62–65, 133–36, etc.

40. Vernon Parrington, *Main Currents in American Thought* (New York, 1930), 3:387–96 (reprinted from 1929 introduction to *Giants*, above note 36).

41. See reviews by James Gray in *Saturday Review of Literature*, April 15, 1939, pp. 11–12, and Percy Hutchison in *New York Times Book Review*, April 15, 1939. Mrs. Rölvaag has left behind a long list of corrections and criticisms (NAHA). A letter from Colcord to Professor Solum (February 10, 1938) expresses considerable dismay at the picture drawn. I will add that Rölvaag's Norwegian passages are handled rather too freely for my taste, often without indicating omissions and telescoping. Documentation is sparse.

42. For the papers of the 1974 symposium, see Thorson, ed., *Ole Rölvaag*. The seminar at Dönna included papers by Ella Valborg Tweet, Gudrun Hovde Gvåle, and Lloyd Hustvedt, and was directed by Jon Austad and Halldor Sandvin. See *Helgelands Blad*, June 26 and 29, 1976. The symposium of 1978 was only partly devoted to Rölvaag; for the papers, see Arthur R. Huseboe and William Geyer, *Where the West Begins* (Sioux Falls, S.D., 1978). See also Huseboe, *Big Sioux Pioneers* (Sioux Falls, S.D., 1980).

43. Carl C. Van Doren, *The American Novel, 1789–1939* (New York, 1940), pp. 301–2.

44. D. N. Curley, M. Kramer, and E. F. Kramer, *Modern American Literature: Library of Literary Criticism of Modern American Literature*, 4th ed., vol. 3 (New York: Ungar, 1969).

45. Robert E. Spiller, et al., *Literary History of the United States*, 4th ed., rev. (New York, 1974), pp. 689–90.

46. Robert Steensma, "The South Dakota Novel: Thoughts after a Centennial," *North Dakota Quarterly* 30 (Spring 1962):40–41.

47. For a thoughtful and informative survey of the conditions and personalities of Scandinavian-American literature, see Dorothy Burton Skårdal, "The Scandinavian Immigrant Writer in America," *Norwegian-American Studies* 21 (1962):14–53.

48. Bojer, *The Emigrants* was reprinted by the University of Nebraska Press in 1978, with a valuable introduction by Paul Reigstad. Unfortunately, the translation was not checked and revised for its many errors; e.g., on p. 1 the word *gauk*, here meaning "scamp," is translated "bootlegger."

49. See, for example, the final paragraph (p. 351).

50. For an excellent account of Moberg's life and work, see Philip Holmes, *Vilhelm Moberg* (Boston: Twayne Publishers, 1980).

51. The titles in English are: *The Emigrants* (1951), *Unto a Good Land* (1957), *The Settlers* (1978), and *The Last Letter Home* (1978). This complete version is published by Popular Library (in paperback).

52. For details on Chisago, see Helge Nelson, *The Swedes and the Swedish Settlements in North America*, 2 vols. (Lund: Royal Humanistic Society of the Sciences, 1943).

53. Gunnar Eidevall, *Vilhelm Mobergs Emigrantepos* (Stockholm: Norstedt, 1974), p. 331. For a discussion of the relationship, see Einar Haugēn, "Rölvaag and Moberg: Some Reflections," *Saga och Sed* (Uppsala) (1982):141–55.

54. Moberg, *Invandrarna*, p. 53; *Unto a Good Land*, p. 28.

55. *Riket Grundlægges*, p. 129; *Giants in the Earth*, p. 385.

56. Sophus Keith Winther, "The Emigrant Theme," *Arizona Quarterly* 34 (1978):31–63.

57. Kjetil A. Flatin, "Historisk Roman—Emigrantroman: Genrespørsmål i tre Norske Verk om Utvandringen til Amerika," *Edda* 64 (1977):157–70.

58. "Anomaly in American Literature," *Literary Digest* 96 (March 10, 1928):28–29.

59. There is now even a journal named *MELUS*, for "Multi-Ethnic Literature of the United States" (vol. 1, 1974).

60. Øverland, "Ole Edvart Rölvaag."

61. Skårdal, *The Divided Heart*.

62. *Amerika-Breve*, p. 171; *Per Smevik*, p. 126.

63. OER, "De der Vest og de her Øst" [Those out West and Those back East], *Tidens Tegn* (Oslo), March 22, 1924.

Selected Bibliography

PRIMARY SOURCES

1. Novels and Short Stories
   A. Published in Minneapolis by Augsburg Publishing House.
Amerika-Breve (Letters from America). 1912. [By "Paal Mörck"].
Paa Glemte Veie (On forgotten paths). 1914. [By "Paal Mörck"].
To Tullinger: Et Billede fra Idag (Two fools: A portrait of our times). 1920.
Længselens Baat (The Boat of Longing). 1921.
Fortællinger og Skildringer (Stories and sketches). n.d. [1932].
   B. Published in Oslo (Kristiania) by Aschehoug & Co.
I De Dage——: Fortælling om Norske Nykommere i Amerika (In those days——
   : A story about Norwegian immigrants in America). 1924. Reprint,
   Den Norske Bokklubben, 1975.
I De Dage——: Riket Grundlægges (Founding the kingdom). 1925. Reprint:
   Den Norske Bokklubben, 1975.
Peder Seier (Peder Victorious). 1928. Reprint: Den Norske Bokklubben,
   1975.
Den Signede Dag (The blessed day). 1931. Reprint. Den Norske Bokklub-
   ben, 1975.
   C. Published in New York and London by Harper & Brothers: English
   translations.
Giants in the Earth: A Saga of the Prairie. Translated by Lincoln Colcord
   and the Author. New York and London: Harper & Brothers, 1927.
   Reprints: Harper's Modern Classics, 1929, introduction by Vernon
   L. Parrington; A. L. Burt, 1930; Blue Ribbon Books, 1937; Harper's
   Modern Classics, 1964, introduction by Jessie Bell Lewis; Harper's
   Torchbooks, 1964, introduction by Einar Haugen; Harper's Perennial
   Classics, 1965.
Peder Victorious: A Tale of the Pioneers Twenty Years Later. Translated by
   Nora O. Solum and the Author. New York and London: Harper &
   Brothers, 1929. Reprints: A. L. Burt, 1931; Harper's Perennial Clas-
   sics, 1966, introduction by Gudrun Hovde Gvåle, translated and
   adapted by Einar Haugen; Greenwood Press, 1973.
Pure Gold. Translated by Sivert Erdahl and the Author. New York and
   London: Harper's, 1930. Reprints: Greenwood Press, 1973. (Nor-

wegian translation: *Rent guld.* Translated by Charles Kent. Oslo: H. Aschehoug, 1932).

Their Father's God. Translated by Trygve M. Ager. New York and London: Harper's, 1931. Reprints: A. L. Burt, 1933; Greenwood Press, 1973.

The Boat of Longing. Translated by Nora O. Solum. New York and London: Harper's 1933. Reprints: A. L. Burt, 1935; Greenwood Press, 1974. D. Published in Minneapolis by Dillon Press.

The Third Life of Per Smevik. Translated by Ella Valborg Tweet and Solveig Zempel. 1971.

2. Nonfiction. (Unless otherwise stated, all are published by Augsburg Publishing House.)

Ordforklaring til Nordahl Rolfsens Læsebok for Folkeskolen, II. (Glossary to Nordahl Rolfsen's reader for the elementary schools, vol. II. Kristiania: Dybwad, 1908.). 1909.

Haandbok i Norsk Retskrivning og Uttale til Skolebruk og Selvstudium (Handbook in Norwegian orthography and pronunciation for school use and home study). With P. J. Eikeland. 1916.

Deklamationsboken (The declamation book). 1918.

Norsk Læsebok (Norwegian reader). 3 vols. With P. J. Eikeland. 1919, 1920, 1925.

Omkring Fædrearven (About our ancestral heritage). Northfield, Minn.: St. Olaf College Press, 1922.

Mindebok om Hans Nielsen Hauge (Memorial volume about Hans Nielsen Hauge). With M. O. Wee. 1926.

3. Articles and Essays (arranged chronologically)

"Hvor Staar Vi Idag med Hensyn til Norsken? Sprogene i Skolerne" (Where are we today with regard to Norwegian? The languages in the schools.). *Skandinaven,* May 24, 25, 27, 1911.

"Billeder fra Nordland" (Pictures from Nordland). *Nord-Norge,* December 1917, pp. 2–6. Storm of January 25, 1893.

"Om den Nye Retskrivning" (About the new orthography). *Lutheraneren* 1 (1917):611–13.

"For Fædrearven" (For our ancestral heritage). Page with this title edited in *Visergutten* (Canton, S.D.) from February 3, 1921 to June 15, 1922, with many essays by Rölvaag.

"Kildahl ved St. Olaf College" (Kildahl at St. Olaf College). In *Dr. John Nathan Kildahl: En Mindebok.* Edited by R. Malmin (Minneapolis: Augsburg, 1921), pp. 125–47.

"Concerning the Value of Being Alone." *Manitou Messenger,* January 10, 1922.

"De der Vest og de her Öst" (Those out West and Those back East). *Tidens Tegn* (Oslo), March 22, 1924.

"Det Norge Jeg Fandt" (The Norway I found). *Decorah-Posten,* November 4, 1924—January 6, 1925.

"Storhavet ved Midtvinterstid" (The ocean at midwinter). *Reform,* April 3, 1924.

"Den Gamle Stua" (The old cottage). *Decorah-Posten,* January 13, 1925.

"The Birth of St. Olaf College." *Lutheran Church Herald,* May 19, 1925, pp. 614–20.

"Om Arven" (On our heritage). Speech at Norse-American Centennial. *Duluth Skandinav,* July 10, 1925 [etc.].

"Hvorfor jeg er medlem af Historielaget" (Why I am a member of the Historical Association). *Lutheraneren* 10 (1926): 326 [etc.]

"Professor Julius E. Olson, a Preacher of Idealism." *Scandinavian Studies* 8 (1925–26):270–74.

"Forord" (Preface). In *Mindebok om Hans Nielsen Hauge.* With M. O. Wee. 1926.

"When a Novelist Is in a Hurry." *Scandinavian Studies* 9 (1926–27):61–67.

"Indvandringens Tragedie" (The tragedy of immigration). *Decorah-Posten,* October 7, 1927.

"Male Students Shun Literary Study; Rölvaag Blames Economic Struggle." *St. Paul Sunday Pioneer Press,* November 17, 1927.

"The Genesis of *Giants in the Earth.*" *Editor* (New York) 78 (August 6, 1927):81–85.

"Foreword." In *Giants in the Earth: A Tragedy in Three Acts and a Prologue,* by Thomas Job. Minneapolis: Northwestern Press, [1929], pp. v–vi.

"Vikings of the Middle West." *American Magazine* 108 (October 1929):44–47, 83, 86.

" 'Pure Gold.' " *Editor,* March 1, 1930, p. 165.

"Christian Doctrine in Ibsen's 'Peer Gynt.' " *Religion in Life* 1 (1932):70–89.

4. Unpublished Writings (In Rölvaag Collection, St. Olaf College; a selected list.)

"Dagbog" (Diary). 1896–1901.

"Fjerde juli 1903." Fourth of July speech, Lime Grove, Nebraska, 1903.

"Nils og Astri" (Nils and Astri). Novel, 1904–5, etc.

"Individualiteten" (Individuality). Commencement oration, St. Olaf College, 1905.

Translation of Nini Roll Anker's play *Kirken* (The church). 1921.

"Books and Folks." Speech at University of Chicago, 1928.

"The Romance of a Life". Unfinished autobiography, 1931.

SECONDARY SOURCES

1. Bibliographies
Andersen, Thor M. *A Bibliography of Norwegian-American Literature.* In press. Oslo: Universitetsbiblioteket. Made available to author in card catalog form.
Bjerke, Robert. "A Rölvaag Bibliography." Unpublished manuscript, 1975–76. Complete listing of published books and shorter literary works. Copy in Rölvaag Collection, NAHA.
Hovde, Oivind M., and Martha E. Henzler, eds. *Norwegian-American Newspapers in Luther College Library.* Decorah, Iowa: Luther College Press, 1975.
Hustvedt, Lloyd. *Guide to Manuscripts Collections of the Norwegian-American Historical Association.* Northfield, Minn.: NAHA, 1979. Lists Rölvaag papers as collection no. 732, with general description of contents. This is supplemented at the archive by a card catalog listing the items and their location.
Johnson, Janet Hovey. "A Bibliography: Ole Edvart Rölvaag 1900–Present." Unpublished manuscript, 1981. Useful, but incomplete.

2. Books and Parts of Books
(All the dissertations and reference works below have bibliographies, which have been checked. Note that in this list, the following types of items have been omitted, unless of unusual interest: interviews, notices of books, obituaries, reminiscences, and reviews of books. Except for major works, items in the Notes and References are also omitted.)
Andersen, Arlow W. *The Norwegian-Americans.* Boston: Twayne Publishers, 1975, p. 171–73. Good popular account of history of immigration.
Blegen, Theodore C. *Norwegian Migration to America 1825–1860.* Northfield, Minn.: NAHA, 1931. Basic research work on early immigration.
————. *Norwegian Migration to America: The American Transition.* Northfield, Minn.: NAHA, 1940. Continues preceding; adds much social history.
Boynton, Percy C. *America in Contemporary Fiction.* Chicago: University of Chicago Press, 1940, pp. 225–40. Chapter on Rölvaag.
Bukdahl, Jörgen. *Det Skjulte Norge.* Copenhagen: Aschehoug, 1926. Essay by noted Danish critic.
Chrislock, Carl H. *Ethnicity Challenged: The Upper Midwest Norwegian-American Experience in World War I.* Topical Studies Series 3. North-

field, Minn.: NAHA, 1981. Story of anti-foreign views as these affected Norwegians.

Colcord, Lincoln. Introduction to *Giants in the Earth*. New York: Harper's, 1927, pp. xi–xxii.

———. "Rölvaag the Fisherman Shook His Fist at Fate." *American Magazine* 105 (March 1928):36–37, 188, 190, 192.

Flanagan, John T., ed. *America Is West*. Minneapolis: University of Minnesota Press, 1945. "Toward the Sunset" from *Giants,* pp. 203–18, with introduction, p. 204.

Gvåle, Gudrun Hovde. *Ole Edvart Rölvaag: Nordmann og Amerikanar*. Oslo: Universitetsforlaget, 1962. Standard biography in Norwegian.

Haugen, Einar. Introduction to *Giants in the Earth*. New York: Harper Torchbook Edition, 1964, pp. ix–xxiii.

———. *The Norwegian Language in America: A Study in Bilingual Behavior*. 2 vols. Philadelphia: University of Pennsylvania Press, 1953. Revised in one volume by Indiana University Press, 1969. Immigrants' language.

———. *Language Conflict and Language Planning: The Case of Modern Norwegian*. Cambridge, Mass.: Harvard University Press, 1966. Norwegian language controversy in twentieth century.

Hetle, Erik. *Lars W. Boe, a Biography*. Minneapolis: Augsburg, 1949. Written by professor of physics, close friend of Rölvaag.

Huseboe, Arthur R., and William Geyer, eds. *Where the West Begins*. Sioux Falls, S.D.: Center for Western Studies Press, 1978. Essays by K. Paulson, N. Eckstein.

———. *Big Sioux Pioneers: Essays about the Settlement of the Dakota Prairie Frontier*. Sioux Falls, S.D.: Nordland Heritage Foundation, 1980. Essays by Carolyn Geyer, Curtis Ruud, and Lloyd Hustvedt.

Jorgenson, Theodore, and Nora O. Solum. *Ole Edvart Rölvaag: A Biography*. New York: Harper's, 1939. Standard biography in English.

Karolides, Nicholas. *The Pioneer in the American Novel, 1900–1950*. Norman: University of Oklahoma Press, 1967. Focusing on Willa Cather and Rölvaag.

Lovoll, Odd S. *A Folk Epic: The Bygdelag in America*. Boston: Twayne Publishers (for NAHA), 1975. Includes Rölvaag's Nordlandslaget.

Lyngstad, Sverre. *Jonas Lie*. Boston: Twayne Publishers, 1977. One of Rölvaag's models.

Meiklejohn, Alexander. *What Does American Mean?* New York: Norton, 1935. *Giants* illustrates his thesis that Americans have substituted love of independence for the love of freedom (145–150).

Meyer, Roy W. *The Middle Western Farm Novel in the Twentieth Century*. Lincoln, Nebr.: Century, 1965, esp. pp. 56–67. "There is little doubt that *Giants in the Earth* is the most satisfying treatment of the pioneering theme that has thus far appeared in the literature of the Middle West, perhaps the finest achievement in the realm of the farm novel."

Morison, Samuel Eliot, and Henry Steele Commager. *The Growth of the American Republic.* 2 vols. 3d ed. New York and London: Oxford University Press, 1942. "*Giants in the Earth* chronicles, as no other volume has, the combination of physical experience which is the warp and woof of the western movement; but instead of its being the proud story of man's conquest of the earth, it is the tragedy of earth's humbling of man." (284).

Murray, John J., ed. *The Heritage of the Middle West.* Norman: University of Oklahoma Press, 1958. "The best of all fictional attempts to picture the coming of the foreigner to the untouched prairie" (John T. Flanagan, p. 226).

Neidle, Cecyle S. *Great Immigrants.* New York: Twayne Publishers, 1973. Rölvaag: "He has given to the American people a legacy that neither time nor changing customs can diminish" (181–202).

Nelson, E. Clifford, and Eugene L. Fevold. *The Lutheran Church among Norwegians.* 2 vols. Minneapolis: Augsburg Publishing House, 1960. Standard, official account.

Parrington, Vernon. Introduction to *Giants in the Earth.* New York: Harper's, 1929, pp. ix–xx. Reprinted in *Main Currents in American Thought,* vol. 3 (New York: Harcourt, Brace, 1930), pp. 387–96. Major American critic.

Qualey, Carlton C. *Norwegian Settlement in the United States.* Northfield, Minn.: NAHA, 1938. Chronology of settlement.

Reaske, Herbert E. *Rölvaag's Giants in the Earth.* Monarch Notes and Study Guides. New York: Monarch Press, 1965. For high schools.

Reigstad, Paul. *Rölvaag: His Life and Art.* Lincoln: University of Nebraska Press, 1972. Valuable account of authorship.

———. "O. E. Rölvaag." *Columbia Dictionary of Modern European Literature.* 2d ed. Edited by J-A Bédé and William B. Edgerton. New York: Columbia University Press, 1980.

Shaw, Joseph M. *History of St. Olaf College 1874–1974.* Northfield, Minn.: St. Olaf College Press, 1974. Standard official account by professor of theology.

Simonson, Harold P. *The Closed Frontier: Studies in American Literary Tragedy.* New York: Holt, Rinehart & Winston, 1970. "The Tragic Trilogy of Ole Rölvaag, 77–97."

Skårdal, Dorothy Burton. *The Divided Heart: Scandinavian Immigrant Experiences through Literary Sources.* Lincoln: University of Nebraska Press, 1974. Thorough survey.

Thorson, Gerald, ed. *Ole Rölvaag: Artist and Cultural Leader.* Northfield, Minn.: St. Olaf College Press, 1975. Papers given at symposium, October 28–29, 1974.

Van Doren, Carl C. *The American Novel, 1789–1939.* New York: MacMillan, 1940, pp. 301–2.

3. Articles (selected)

Ager, Waldemar. "Ole Edvart Rölvaag." Introduction to O. E. Rölvaag, *Fortællinger og Skildringer,* pp. 7–32. [Translated by Solveig P. Tweet, unpublished, 1969.]

Baker, Joseph E. "Western Man against Nature: *Giants in the Earth.*" *College English* 4 (1942):19–26. On Rölvaag.

Bjork, Kenneth O. "The Unknown Rölvaag: Secretary in the Norwegian-American Historical Association." *Norwegian-American Studies and Records* 11 (1940):114–49.

————. "Literature in Its Relation to Norwegian-American History." *Scandinavian Studies* 38 (1966):13–19. By a Rölvaag student who became professor of history at St. Olaf and editor of the NAHA.

————. "The Norwegians in America. 'Giants in the Earth.'" In *The Immigrant Experience in America.* Edited by Frank J. Copra and Thomas J. Curran. Boston: Twayne Publishers, 1976, pp. 63–94.

Boewe, Charles. "Rölvaag's America: An Immigrant Novelist's Views." *Western Humanities Review* 11 (1957):3–12.

Boynton, Percy H. "O. E. Rölvaag and the Conquest of the Pioneer." *English Journal* 18 (1929):535–42. Eminent American critic.

Carlin, Jerome. "Twelve Days with *Giants in the Earth.*" *High Points: In the Work of the High Schools of New York City* 40, no. 1 (January 1956):5–18.

Chrislock, Carl H. "Name Change and the Church 1918–1920." *Norwegian-American Studies* 27 (1977):194–223.

Eckstein, Neil T. "The Social Criticism of Ole Edvart Rölvaag." *Norwegian-American Studies* 24 (1970):112–36.

————. "O. E. Rölvaag: The Marginality of the Bi-cultural Writer." In *Ole Rölvaag.* Edited by Gerald Thorson. Northfield, Minn.: St. Olaf College Press, 1975, pp. 65–68.

————. "*Giants in the Earth* as Saga." In *Where the West Begins.* Edited by A. Huseboe and W. Geyer. Sioux Falls, S.D.: Center for Western Studies Press, 1978, pp. 34–41. Essay by American historian.

Flatin, Kjetil A. "Historisk Roman—Emigrantroman: Genrespørsmål i tre Norske Verk om Utvandringen til Amerika." *Edda* 64 (1977):157–70. Essay by Norwegian critic.

Fox, Maynard. "The Bearded Face Set toward the Sun." *Ball State Teacher's College Forum* 1 (1961):62–64.

Geyer, Carolyn. "An Introduction to Ole Rölvaag (1876–1931)." In *Big Sioux Pioneers*. Edited by Arthur Huseboe. Sioux Falls, S.D.: Nordland Heritage Foundation, 1980, pp. 54–62.

Goldstein, Sidney. "The Death of Per Hansa." *English Journal* 56 (1967):464–66.

Hahn, Steve. "Vision and Reality in *Giants in the Earth.*" *South Dakota Review* 17 (1979):85–100.

Haugen, Einar. "O. E. Rölvaag: Norwegian-American." *Norwegian-American Studies and Records* 7 (1933):53–73.

Haugen, Kristine. "Glimt fra Rölvaags Liv." *Decorah-Posten,* December 8, 1931. Obituary based on personal letters.

Heitmann, John. "Ole Edvart Rölvaag." *Norwegian-American Studies and Records* 12 (1941):144–66. For a fuller version, see *Decorah-Posten,* August 15, 22, 29, 1941.

Helgeland, John. "Beret's Problem: An Essay on Immigrant Pioneer Religion." *Lutheran Quarterly* 28 (1976):45–53.

Hibbard, Addison. "Analysis of O. E. Rölvaag's *Pure Gold.*" *Creative Reading* 4 (1930):153–69.

Hustvedt, Lloyd. "The Simon Johnson-Ole Edvart Rölvaag Correspondence." In *Norwegian Influence on the Upper Midwest.* Edited by Harald Naess. Duluth: University of Minnesota-Duluth, 1976, pp. 54–58.

———. "Values in Rölvaag's Trilogy." In *Big Sioux Pioneers.* Edited by Arthur Huseboe. Sioux Falls, S.D.: Nordland Heritage Foundation, 1980, pp. 79–88.

Jordahl, Owen W. "Folkloristic Influences upon Rölvaag's Youth." *Western Folklore* 34 (January 1975):1–15. From a dissertation of 1972.

Jorgenson, Theodore. "The Main Factors in Rölvaag's Authorship." *Norwegian-American Studies and Records* 10 (1938):135–51. Summary by Rölvaag's successor and biographer.

Larsen, Erling. "The Art of O. E. Rölvaag." *Minnesota English Journal* 8 (1972):17–29.

Laverty, Carroll D. "Rölvaag's Creation of the Sense of Doom in *Giants in the Earth.*" *South Central Bulletin* 27, no. 4 (1967):45–48.

Meldrum, Barbara. "Fate, Sex, and Naturalism in Rölvaag's Trilogy." In *Ole Rölvaag.* Edited by Gerald Thorson. Northfield, Minn.: St. Olaf College Press, 1975, pp. 41–49.

Mortensen, Wayne F. "The Problem of the Loss of Culture in Rölvaag's *Giants in the Earth, Peder Victorious,* and *Their Father's God.*" *Minnesota English Journal* 8 (1972):42–50.

Moseley, Ann. "The Land as Metaphor in Two Scandinavian Immigrant Novels." *MELUS* 5 (1978):33–38. *Giants* and Winther's *Take All to Nebraska.*

Mossberg, Christer Lennart. "Shucking the Pastoral Ideal." In *Where the West Begins.* Edited by A. Huseboe and W. Geyer. Sioux Falls, S.D.: Center for Western Studies Press, 1978, pp. 42–50.

Överland, Orm. "Ole Edvart Rölvaag and *Giants in the Earth:* A Writer Between Two Countries." *American Studies in Scandinavia* (Oslo) 13 (1981):35–45.

————. "Ole Edvart Rölvaag og den Norske Kulturen i Amerika." Forthcoming. Essays by Norwegian-Americanist.

Paulson, Kristoffer F. "Rölvaag as Prophet: The Tragedy of Americanization." In *Ole Rölvaag.* Edited by Gerald Thorson. Northfield, Minn.: St. Olaf College Press, 1975, pp. 57–64.

————. "Berdahl Family History and Rölvaag's Immigrant History." *Norwegian-American Studies and Records* 27 (1977):55–76. Personal sources of *Giants.*

————. "Ole Rölvaag, Herbert Krause, and the Frontier Thesis of Frederick Jackson Turner." In *Where the West Begins.* Edited by A. Huseboe and W. Geyer. Sioux Falls, S.D.: Center for Western Studies Press, 1978, pp. 24–33.

————. "What Was Lost: Ole Rölvaag's *The Boat of Longing.*" *MELUS* 7 (1980):51–60.

[Reiff], Raychel Ann Haugrud. "Rölvaag's Search for Soria Moria." *Norwegian-American Studies* 26 (1974):103–17. Based on dissertation, see below.

————. "Nils Vaag: Human Soul in Search of the Perfect." In *Ole Rölvaag.* Edited by Gerald Thorson. Northfield, Minn.: St. Olaf College Press, 1975, pp. 33–40.

Reigstad, Paul. "Rölvaag as Myth-maker." In *Ole Rölvaag.* Edited by Gerald Thorson. Northfield, Minn.: St. Olaf College Press, 1975, pp. 51–55.

Rölvaag, Ella Valborg. See Tweet.

Ruud, Curtis D. "Beret and the Prairie in *Giants in the Earth.*" *Norwegian-American Studies* 28 (1979):217–44.

————. "Rölvaag, the Ash Lad, and New and Old World Values." In *Big Sioux Pioneers.* Edited by Arthur Huseboe. Sioux Falls, S.D.: Nordland Heritage Foundation, 1980, pp. 63–78. Based on dissertation in 1977, see below.

Scholes, Robert. "The Fictional Heart of the Country: From Rölvaag to Gass." In *Ole Rölvaag.* Edited by Gerald Thorson. Northfield, Minn.: St. Olaf College Press, 1975, pp. 1–13.

Semmingsen, Ingrid. "Commentary to Gvåle: *Rölvaag.*" *Edda* 53 (1966):381–98. Critique of dissertation.

Simonson, Harold P. "Rölvaag and Kierkegaard." *Scandinavian Studies* 49 (1977):67–80. Philosophical essay by professor of English.

————. "*Angst* on the Prairie: Reflections on Immigrants, Rölvaag, and Beret." *Norwegian-American Studies* 29 (1983):89–110. Critique of Turner's thesis.

Skårdal, Dorothy Burton. "The Scandinavian Immigrant Writer in America." *Norwegian-American Studies* 21 (1962):14–53. Essay by Americanist at University of Oslo.

————. "Commentary on Gvåle: *Rölvaag*." *Edda* 53 (1966):398–402. Critique of dissertation.

Skard, Sigmund. "Commentary on Gvåle, *Rölvaag*." *Edda* 53 (1966):361–80. Critique of dissertation.

Smemo, Kenneth. "The Norwegian Ethnic Experience and the Literature of Waldemar Ager." In *Norwegian Influence on the Upper Midwest.* Edited by Harald Naess. Duluth: University of Minnesota-Duluth, 1976, pp. 59–64. On Rölvaag's literary rival.

Solum, Nora O. "The Sources of the Rölvaag Biography." *Norwegian-American Studies and Records* 11 (1940):150–59. Important information by co-author of biography.

Steensma, Robert. "Rölvaag and Turner's Frontier Thesis." *North Dakota Quarterly* 27 (1959):100–104.

Stevens, Robert L. " 'Pure Gold': An Appreciation." In *Ole Rölvaag.* Edited by Gerald Thorson. Northfield, Minn.: St. Olaf College Press, 1975, pp. 25–31.

Storm, Melvin. "The Immigrant in *Giants in the Earth:* Conflict and Resolution." *Heritage of Kansas* 8 (1975):36–40.

Strandvold, Georg. "Rölvaags Præriesaga." *Decorah-Posten,* December 11, 1931–January 29, 1932. Criticism of the Norwegian version of *Giants* by Danish-American editor.

Suderman, Elmer F. "An Experiment in Reading *Giants in the Earth. Minnesota English Journal* 8 (1972):30–41.

Thorson, Gerald. "Ole Edvart Rölvaag: 1876–1931." *MELUS* 3, no. 3 (1976):6–7.

Tweet, Ella Valborg (née Rölvaag). "My Father." *American Prefaces* 1 (1936):105–8. Valuable family reminiscences.

————. Introduction to *The Third Life of Per Smevik,* pp. vii–xxiv.

————. "Recollections of My Father, O. E. Rölvaag," *Minnesota English Journal* 8 (1972):4–16.

Winther, Sophus Keith. "The Emigrant Theme." *Arizona Quarterly* 34 (1978):31–63.

4. Dissertations and Theses

Anderson, Carol Jean. "Narrative Techniques in Selected Novels by Ole Edvart Rölvaag." Ph.D. dissertation, University of Arkansas, 1979.

Eckstein, Neil T. "The Marginal Man as Novelist: The Norwegian-American Writers, H. H. Boyesen and O. E. Rölvaag, as Critics of American Institutions." Ph.D. dissertation, University of Pennsylvania, 1965.

Geyer, Carolyn. "Beret in the Prairie Trilogy of Ole E. Rölvaag: A Study of Character Relationships." M.A. thesis, Auburn University, 1965.

Halvorson, Hazel L. "The Norwegian Heritage in America: Rölvaag's Concern for a Pluralistic Society." M.A. thesis, South Dakota State University, 1974.

Jordahl, Owen W. "Three Essays on Ole E. Rölvaag." M.A. thesis, University of Utah, 1972. See article above.

Phenneger, Richard Ernest. "The Problems of Self-Realization in the Novels of O. E. Rölvaag." M.A. thesis, Washington State College, 1954.

[Reiff], Raychel Ann Haugrud. "In Quest of Soria Moria: The Search for Happiness in O. E. Rölvaag's Characters." Ph.D. dissertation, University of Utah, 1971 *(Dissertation Abstracts* 32, 1974, no. 1474A). See articles above.

Reigstad, Paul M. "The Art and Mind of Ole Edvart Rölvaag." Ph.D. dissertation, University of New Mexico, 1958. See book above.

Ruud, Curtis. "The Dakota Prairie as Changing Force in Ole E. Rölvaag's *Giants in the Earth.*" Ph.D. dissertation, University of Nebraska, 1977 *(Dissertation Abstracts* 38, 1978, no. 7337a–38A). See articles above.

Sörheim, Aashild. "To Fedreland Eller Intet? Emigrant-Problemet Slik O. E. Rölvaag har Fremstilt det i Romanserien 'I De Dage.' " Hovedopgave til Nordisk Hovedfag, University of Oslo, 1977.

Steensma, Robert. "Ole Edvart Rölvaag: A Critical Study of His Norwegian-American Novels." Ph.D. dissertation, University of Illinois, 1955.

Stevens, Robert Lowell. "Ole Edvart Rölvaag: A Critical Study of His Norwegian-American Novels." Ph.D. dissertation, University of Illinois, 1955 (Doctoral Dissertation Series no. 15,276).

Thorson, Gerald H. "America Is Not Norway: The Story of the Norwegian-American Novel." Ph.D. dissertation, Columbia University, 1957.

Tyler, Frances Lawrence. "O. E. Rölvaag: His Place in American Literature." M.A. thesis, University of Missouri, 1950.

Vettore, Lavinia. "From Saga to Psychological Drama: *Giants in the Earth.*" Dissertation, University of Venice (Italy), 1981.

Index

(Excluding front matter, footnotes, and bibliography)

DATE DUE

DEMCO 38-297